TWILIGHT OF INNOCENCE

TRUE CRIME SERIES
Albert Borowitz, Editor

Terrorism for Self-Glorification: The Herostrotos Syndrome
Albert Borowitz

Tracks to Murder
Jonathan Goodman

Twilight of Innocence: The Disappearance of Beverly Potts
James Jessen Badal

TWILIGHT OF INNOCENCE

The Disappearance of Beverly Potts

James Jessen Badal

The Kent State University Press

KENT & LONDON

© 2005 by The Kent State University Press, Kent, Ohio 44242

ALL RIGHTS RESERVED

Library of Congress Catalog Card Number 2004027926

ISBN 0-87338-836-4

Manufactured in the United States of America

09 08 07 06 05   5 4 3 2 1

Designed by Christine Brooks and set in Stone Serif and Nuptial Script.
Printed by Sheridan Books, Inc., of Ann Arbor, Michigan.

Library of Congress Cataloging-in-Publication Data

Badal, James Jessen, 1943–

Twilight of innocence : the disappearance of Beverly Potts /
James Jessen Badal.

p. cm. —(True crime series)

Includes bibliographical references and index.

ISBN 0-87338-836-4 (pbk. : alk. paper) ∞

1. Potts, Beverly Rose, 1941–

2. Missing children—Ohio—Cleveland—Case studies.

3. Abduction—Ohio—Cleveland—Case studies.

4. Missing persons—Investigation—Ohio—Cleveland—Case studies.

I. Title. II. True crime series (Kent, Ohio)

HV6762.U5B33 2005

364.15'4'0977132—dc22

2004027926

British Library Cataloging-in-Publication data are available.

In memory of Beverly Rose Potts

And for my partners:
Anita, BobW, and Mark

Your mind goes back. We were standing in a circle playing some game with a ball. She [Beverly] was holding a ball—something like a basketball—and she was weaving back and forth.

Donna Kensick, one of Beverly's classmates, in a summer 2002 interview.

Contents

Preface and Acknowledgments

Not everyone thought this book was such a good idea. First of all, however poignant the disappearance of Beverly Potts may be, was there enough information in her story, doubters wondered, to justify an entire book? Second, who would want a "true crime" study with no satisfactory solution? And unless I got extraordinarily lucky, there would be none. My previous book, *In the Wake of the Butcher: Cleveland's Torso Murders,* may not have solved the Kingsbury Run butcheries, but at least— so ran the argument—I was dealing with a series of gruesome murders that, against the ugly background of inner-city Cleveland life in the 1930s, hooked readers through the unspeakable brutality of the butcheries, and then nailed them with some very disturbing morgue and crime-scene photographs. The disappearance of Beverly Potts simply did not provide an opportunity for such graphic horrors. Instead of the appalling shantytowns that spread through Cleveland's industrial areas in the Flats and reached into Kingsbury Run, the prehistoric riverbed south of the city, where many decapitated and otherwise butchered corpses were discovered, I could offer only a 1950s working-class Cleveland neighborhood—neat, clean, and utterly normal in every way. In place of dismembered body parts, I could provide only photographs of neighborhood parents and children—the vague, telltale signs of worry and confusion in their eyes the sole indication that anything was amiss. The Kingsbury Run murders also embraced a substantial number of victims and went on, possibly, for more than a decade, pounding the city with a series of repeated shocks. Not only was the disappearance of Beverly Potts an isolated, single event, she vanished in an instant; there were few witnesses and no clues as to her ultimate fate. There was nothing but the grinding frustration of an official investigation that lurched forward in

ix

fits and starts for more than fifty years, leaving behind the memory of a little girl who continues to haunt Cleveland a half century later.

To those who gave their unqualified support from the very beginning, I offer my deepest gratitude. Special thanks to the Kent State University Press. As the publishers of many fine historical studies, especially on the American Civil War, the people at the Press realize that history can often be messy, even inconclusive—certainly nowhere near as neat and precise as we would like it to be. While working on *Twilight of Innocence,* I was never under any pressure to make events more sensational than they already were; nor was I ever asked to tie up loose ends that stubbornly insisted on dangling or to make speculations with which I was not entirely comfortable or that could not be fully supported by the facts.

After the publication of a book, I imagine most authors experience a combination of exhilaration and exhaustion—a brief, though emotionally chaotic, period during which no sane person would ever think seriously of starting another such project. My special thanks to John Hubbell, former director of the Press. Though well aware of my still-agitated state, he cautiously encouraged me to proceed—"If you think you're up to it"—when I first relayed the Beverly Potts idea to him before the ink on my previous book was even dry. Thanks also to Joanna Craig for her constant good humor, sensitivity, patience, and enthusiasm—and for uttering those wonderful, magical words when I initially pitched my Beverly Potts proposal to her: "We want this book."

Thanks to James Jaros, former dean of humanities at the Eastern Campus of Cuyahoga Community College, for supporting my application for a sabbatical leave during the 2002–03 academic year to do the major research necessary, and sincerest thanks to the college's Professional Improvement Leave Committee for granting my request.

Special thanks to Anita Potts. She was twenty-two when her ten-year-old sister, Beverly, suddenly vanished in 1951 without leaving a trace. By all contemporary accounts, it was her strength that held the Potts household together in the desperate days following her sister's disappearance. She kept a watchful eye on her grieving parents and played hostess to the legions of neighbors, other well-wishers, police, and reporters who tramped in and out of the family home at 11304 Linnet Avenue. Anita Potts compelled the admiration of everyone, especially *Cleveland Press* staff reporter Ben Marino, who came in contact with her during the dark days of the investigation. She generously offered me her full cooperation even though that meant revisiting an unspeakably painful episode in her own life and the life of her family. I have lost track of the conflicts in the case record that she clarified or otherwise straightened out—in spite of her insistence that her memory is not as good as it used to be. She also rummaged through what she jokingly referred to as her "debris," unearthing some wonderful family photographs, a number of which appear in this book, as well as some poignant documents and letters that touch on her sister's brief life. I remain deeply grateful for her willing participation.

Among the impressions Anita Potts has carried with her from that nightmarish episode fifty years ago, the memories of city newspaper reporters turning her parents' home into a makeshift command post, with little or no regard for her family's grief and yearning for privacy, remain especially bitter. "I thought it was horrendous," she fumed recently. "The reporters seemed to have no regard for our family." Consequently, she has shunned the public eye and reserved her thoughts about her sister and her inexplicable disappearance for the inner circle of her own family for more than half a century. In November 2003, however, she bravely consented to a recorded interview with producer and director Mark Wade Stone of Storytellers Media Group, Limited, for a documentary about Beverly's baffling case. Many of the remarks and observations attributed to her that appear in this book were culled from the raw footage of that hour-long session. Special thanks to my good friend and collaborator Mark Wade Stone for granting me full access to this material.

Doris O'Donnell Beaufait, former writer and reporter for both the *Cleveland News* and the *Cleveland Plain Dealer,* called me out of the blue one day to tell me how much she enjoyed my book *In the Wake of the Butcher*—a wonderfully generous gesture under any circumstances, but especially so considering her "Uncle Marty" (one-time Cuyahoga County Sheriff Martin L. O'Donnell) did not emerge from *Butcher's* pages in the most favorable light. At a time when female newspaper reporters were still something of a rarity outside the society pages, she built an extraordinary career in Cleveland, covering virtually every big story in the city from her first day on the job. Her knowledge of Cleveland political history and local crimes is encyclopedic; her fund of colorful stories and reminiscences about the major players in the city's life and her ink-stained colleagues on the police beat remains fathoms-deep. She was among the first reporters outside the Potts home in the days following Beverly's disappearance, and she willingly shared her memories and impressions with me. She was also able to rescue little bits of history by attaching names to previously unidentified individuals in old newspaper photographs. "I'm going to be a monumental pain in the butt for you until I'm done with the research," I told her. "That's OK," she retorted—even though at the time she was deeply engaged in writing her memoirs for the Kent State University Press. "Call me anytime." As the only newspaper reporter I could find who covered the Potts case directly, her input was invaluable.

Detective Robert Wolf of the Cleveland Police Department grew up in the shadow of the Beverly Potts story, having spent his early childhood in the same neighborhood from which she so mysteriously vanished. In 2000 he was handed an anonymous letter—a confession of sorts dealing with the Potts case that had shown up in the editorial office of the *Plain Dealer*—and assigned to find out whatever he could about the strange document and its writer. For the next year and a half he chipped away at the haunting case that he had known about since his youth. We walked through Halloran Park and the adjacent Linnet Avenue neighborhood together, studied maps of the area, and discussed in detail the information in the surviving police reports. He pointed out potential leads that should have been checked further but weren't. He encouraged me to be both open-minded and critical, to never dismiss a piece of information out of hand, but at the same time to constantly ask questions. He taught me how to operate like a trained investigator—how to think like a cop.

Thanks to Cleveland police chief Edward Lohn for granting me access to the Beverly Potts case files. I am also grateful to Joseph M. Petkac (officer in charge, Homicide Unit, Cleveland Police Department) and to the men and women under his command for providing me a cubbyhole in which to go over the fragile documents, for showing me where the coffee and the men's room were, and for making me feel entirely welcome.

Thanks to all those who helped in ways both large and small through their willing cooperation: Judith A. Barker (assistant professor of psychology, Cuyahoga Community College, Eastern Campus); William Becker (archivist, *Cleveland Press* Collection, Cleveland State University); Robert Cermak (Cleveland Police Department, retired, and former chairman of the board of trustees, Cleveland Police Historical Society); Nikhil Chand (academic LAN systems specialist, Technology Learning Center, Cuyahoga Community College, Eastern Campus); Kathy Fana (office supervisor at the Cuyahoga County Morgue); John Fransen (Cleveland Police Department, retired); Marge Geiger; Robert J. Georges; David

Holcombe (curator and director, Cleveland Police Historical Society Museum); Glenda L. Hopkins records manager, Cuyahoga County Archives); Richard Karberg; Fred G. Krause; Brent Larkin (director of the *Cleveland Plain Dealer*'s editorial pages); Johnny Little (information support specialist, Technology Learning Center, Cuyahoga Community College, Eastern Campus); Delmar O'Hare (volunteer, Cleveland Police Historical Society Museum); John Panza; Denise L. Reeves (Cleveland Police Department); Larry Rutherford (Cleveland Police Department, retired, and chairman of the board of trustees, Cleveland Police Historical Society); Bill Salupo (Cleveland Police Department); Michaelene M. Taliano (Cleveland Police Department, retired); Donna J. Trocano (nee Kensick) and the family of the late James A. Trocano; Barbara Wilson (assistant manager, Technology Learning Center, Cuyahoga Community College, Eastern Campus); and Kenneth A. Zirm (attorney-at-law, Walter and Haverfield). My thanks also to the staffs of the Cleveland Public Library, the Cleveland State University Library, and the Western Reserve Historical Society Library. Finally, as always seems the case in sensitive matters such as this, there were sources that preferred not to be identified. My thanks to them also.

Introduction

"So, are you starting a new career as a true crime writer?" My answer
was swift and decisive. "No!" I was sitting across the table from staff
reporter Brian Albrecht and a *Cleveland Plain Dealer* photographer in a
depressingly anonymous and sterile room in the *Plain Dealer* building,
giving the first of what would turn out to be many interviews following
the publication of my book *In the Wake of the Butcher: Cleveland's Torso
Murders* (Kent State University Press, 2001). The 250-plus-page volume
that lay between us represented more than ten years of constant, obsessive digging—work that was always grueling, often emotionally drain-
ing; I had no intention of going through it all again. I politely brushed
off questions as to what my next project might be with the same prepared, joking response: "I don't know enough about anything else to
write another book."

Then came a talk and book signing the following June at Lakeview
Cemetery next to the Eliot Ness monument. "Why don't you do Beverly
Potts?" asked one of the more than two hundred attendees. My stock
reply rolled out as it always did, but, inexplicably, I did not reject the
idea out of hand in my own mind as I had so many other suggestions. I
knew the name, of course; what Clevelander didn't? She was a part of
the city's grim folklore: the little girl with the wide-set Bambi eyes who
vanished from her West Side neighborhood in the summer of 1951 as
mysteriously and completely as if she had been abducted on an episode
of *The X-Files*. For decades, her unknown but clearly tragic fate provided
Cleveland parents with an effective club for compelling strict adherence
by their children to family curfews. Her shadow fell across the child-
hoods of virtually every Clevelander of my generation. A colleague at
Cuyahoga Community College remembers checking the bushes outside

A warm glow of nostalgia reminiscent of Norman Rockwell's America. Beverly Potts in 1946. Courtesy of Anita Potts Georges.

her home to see if the missing child all the adults in her life were talking about might be there; a friend from my college days recalls searching up and down the streets of her neighborhood for the little girl she didn't even know. Paul Konet, then a twelve-year-old East Sider, had crossed the Cuyahoga River to visit his friend Bob Ladavac, who lived near Halloran Park. The two boys romped in the playground on the afternoon of August 24, 1951, and watched the show staged there that evening. Paul spent the night at the Ladavac house. When he returned home the next morning, completely oblivious to what had transpired during the night, he found himself placed under virtual house arrest by his worried parents. His story remains typical. If you said "Beverly Potts" to any of my contemporaries, you always got the same response. "My God! My mother wouldn't let me out of the house for months."

With my interest piqued for reasons I did not fully recognize or understand at the time, I began making a series of perfunctory forays into the details of the almost legendary fifty-year-old disappearance. Suddenly, in the spring and summer of 2002, public awareness of abducted children rose to phenomenal heights. There seemed a veritable explosion of kidnappings and near kidnappings on both the local and national levels—though the authorities argued that the number of reported abductions had not increased, only the media attention they received. Five-year-old Samantha Runnion vanished from her Southern California neighborhood, only to be found dead in the desert a few days later. In a case that caught the attention of press and public alike, Elizabeth Smart was snatched at gunpoint from the bedroom of her Utah home while her younger sister watched in disbelieving horror. Immediately, the victim's angelic face flashed across the nation's newspapers and TV screens, a portfolio of family photos and video tapes turning Elizabeth Smart into one of the most instantly recognizable teenagers in the entire country. Her parents grieved and prayed before a national audience; night after night on the evening news, the country watched a somber army of determined searchers prowl the mountainous areas near the Smart home. Almost miraculously, the fourteen-year-old girl turned up alive nine months later. The details of her tortured, nearly yearlong captivity in the hands of a scruffy religious fanatic and his mentally disturbed wife fascinated the entire nation to such a degree that the Smart family found themselves making the rounds of the TV news magazine shows, and Elizabeth watched from the sidelines while Hollywood turned her bizarre ordeal into a made-for-TV movie.

In the Cleveland area, a rash of abductions, attempted abductions, and child murders suddenly grabbed the attention of the local media. Amidst circumstances that eerily echo the disappearance of Beverly Potts, Kristen Jackson of Wooster vanished in September 2002 from the Wayne County fair, and no one in the huge, milling crowds saw a thing. Within about a week, pieces of her dismembered body would be found in a nearby wooded area. In mid-September 2003 eleven-year-old Shakira Johnson inexplicably disappeared from a neighborhood gathering in honor of a slain civil rights activist on East 106 Street. She had come to the gathering with her two brothers, but neither of them saw what happened to her—nor, apparently, did anyone else in the large milling crowd. The sight of Shakira's bright eyes and pixie smile flashing from local TV screens and gracing the pages of the *Plain Dealer* immediately galvanized the entire city. Suddenly, the unknown fate of the little girl waged daily battle in the local media with the war in Iraq for the hearts and minds of Clevelanders; she had become everyone's child. On September 23 the *Plain Dealer* assured anxious city residents that no fewer than forty Cleveland police detectives and FBI agents were combing the area.

Caught firmly in the bright eye of media attention, Shakira's worried mother wavered unsteadily between hope and despair. It seemed as if the entire city, from Mayor Jane Campbell and Cuyahoga County Prosecutor William Mason to Shakira's elementary school classmates, had become involved in the desperate search.

Thanks to an anonymous tip a month later, police found the badly decomposed and mutilated body of a little girl in the weeds close to a derelict building on the city's near east side. But Cleveland would have to wait in agony longer than is usually the case for the coroner's identification. In her eleven years of life, Shakira had never been to a dentist; there were no dental records to match with the dead girl's teeth. When news of the positive ID hit, all of Cleveland and its surrounding suburbs mourned. Immediately and spontaneously, city residents turned the rusty chain-link fence surrounding the vacant field and abandoned warehouse where her body had been discovered into a makeshift memorial for Shakira Johnson. People of every race, religion, and economic circumstance—many from outside the city—made the melancholy pilgrimage to the shrine on East 71 Street. Every evening, local TV reporters stood before the wall of flowers, cards, and stuffed animals with the sort of hushed dignity usually reserved for a church service. Clearly moved, perhaps even awed, by the spectacle of grief unfolding before their cameras, they whispered their reports into their microphones as Clevelanders came together to mourn for the murdered little girl. By mid-November, police had arrested and charged Daniel Hinds, a twenty-five-year-old self-employed handyman, with the kidnapping and murder of Shakira Johnson. In the midst of this unfolding tragedy, on October 21, 2003, the *Plain Dealer* reminded city residents that none of this was new; Cleveland had been through all of it before. "Yesterday's news that a body found last week was Shakira Johnson brought back memories of a ten-year-old girl who also vanished not far from home. . . . Fifty-two years have passed," the paper reflected sadly, "since Cleveland was consumed by the name Beverly Potts."

And the city had, indeed, been consumed—consumed by a disappearance that seemed to defy explanation. No trace of her was ever found. In the hours after she vanished, it wasn't clear that this was anything more than a garden-variety case of a runaway, yet the Cleveland Police Department's chief of detectives was heading up the search. Her case was never officially declared a homicide, yet the head of the homicide department began working on the investigation within a week of her disappearance. Beverly Potts remained the primary occupation of the police until the murder of Marilyn Sheppard overshadowed her three years later. But for the next fifty years, whenever a young Cleveland girl was murdered or inexplicably disappeared, newspapers inevitably compared her to Beverly Potts. For the press and public, any abandoned house or "suspicious" discovery in the neighborhoods close to her Linnet Avenue home was sufficient to revive memories of that shy little girl who smiles demurely from a small handful of surviving photographs.

Though any unsolved case naturally generates a certain allure, Beverly Potts and her fate would seem a poor stepchild in the presence of the city's more glamorous and infamous mysteries. Her story possesses neither the soap-opera sensationalism of the Marilyn Sheppard case nor the sheer brutal horror of the Kingsbury Run murders—the infamous cycle of unsolved decapitation murders that terrified the city in the mid-1930s. Missing children have also become a numbing reality of contemporary life; their photographs slip into our mailboxes, stare at us from milk cartons and post-office walls, confront us from our television screens. Is it conceivable that abducted or murdered children simply were not that common fifty years ago? Neither Beverly nor her family was touched with the sort of celebrity that normally would compel such ruthless media attention. Her father, a stagehand at the Allen Theater in Cleveland, was an average working man; her mother was an utterly unremarkable housewife. This was not the Lindbergh kidnapping. And Cleveland has had its share of more contemporary news-grabbing murders and kidnappings to contend with; there were Tiffany Papish in 1980 and Amy Milhaljevic in 1989. Yet the memory of Beverly Potts endures. Her gentle grip on Cleveland's awareness has never loosened. In the summer of 2001, fifty years after she vanished, an anonymous writer was sending disturbing letters to *Plain Dealer* columnist Brent Larkin claiming to be her abductor and murderer. What is there about this one missing little girl that has kept her story so haunting and compelling for more than half a century?

The circumstances surrounding her disappearance baffled police fifty years ago and remain equally perplexing today: a pleasant late summer evening, a middle-class neighborhood adjacent to a busy north-south street, a public park within five minutes of her Linnet Avenue home, filled that night with a crowd (estimated to number close to fifteen hundred) of children and adults—some presumably her neighbors, friends, and schoolmates—watching a show. And yet she was gone. Police at the time marveled that so many saw so little; in spite of a flurry of reported sightings of little girls all over the city in the days after Beverly's disappearance, only a few acquaintances, both close and casual, actually saw the missing ten-year-old at Halloran Park on the night of August 24, 1951. "I cannot remember any case where there was so little evidence for such a long period of time," lamented the deeply frustrated chief of detectives, James E. McArthur, the officer in charge of the case, to the *Cleveland Press* on August 27.

Beverly Potts's disappearance clearly touched a very raw public nerve, triggering an extraordinary effort on the part of the police. Every city official, including Mayor Thomas A. Burke and Safety Director Alvin J. Sutton, seemed consumed with the case. Though it remains a little difficult to separate the truth from the journalistic hype, all three Cleveland dailies dubbed the search one of the largest and most intense in city history. On August 28 the *Cleveland News* proclaimed, "The army of searchers—the firemen, detectives, police, the city's park and service division employes [*sic*], Civil Air Patrol and neighbors" constituted "Cleveland's most concentrated search in history." The next day, the paper declared that the hunt for Beverly was, indeed, "nationwide." The *Plain Dealer* maintained on August 27 that "inquiries were sent as far afield as Arizona and West Virginia," and the next morning, in a statement remarkably close to the *News*'s assertion on the same day, the *Plain Dealer* insisted that "2000 other searchers, policemen, city service and property employees, Boy Scouts and members of the Civil Air Patrol" searched for the missing girl. On Thursday, August 30, the *Plain Dealer* declared that police received as many as fifteen hundred calls a day regarding Beverly's disappearance: "No missing-person case in Cleveland police history ever aroused a sustained public response comparable to that touched off by the disappearance Friday night of 10-year-old Beverly Potts." On August 27 the *Press* assured anxious city residents that "McArthur already had turned loose the greatest out-pouring of manpower in recent Cleveland history." "Beverly's case may be the only ont [*sic*] of its kind in Cleveland police history," the *Plain Dealer* assured its readers on September 4. "It is unique thus far, because nothing has been learned of the child's fate despite one of the biggest hunts and investigations ever known here." Even as late as December 12, 1955, the *Plain Dealer* declared, "The disappearance rocked Greater Cleveland as have few mysteries in police annals. Repercussion reached from coast to coast."

The scope of the investigation was certainly huge, and neither the dedication nor the professional skill of those involved can be doubted for a second. Fifteen years before in the mid-1930s, however, Cleveland police had mounted an equally large and extraordinary all-out search for the Butcher of Kingsbury Run, a massive effort crippled in part by a simple lack of understanding at the time of the serial-killer dynamic. Could the situation in that summer of 1951 have been similar? Based on what authorities now know about the profile of the typical kidnapper or sexual predator, how effective or appropriate were those police actions fifty years ago?

The local press played a huge role in carving out a permanent niche for Beverly Potts in the city's memory. From the time she vanished on August 24, 1951, newspapers seized on her disappearance with a ferocity that recalled the Lindbergh case. Her story and the subsequent investigation competed with the Korean War for attention on the front pages of city newspapers, winning the confrontation an astonishing number of times. Beverly disappeared on the evening of August 24, and both the *Press* and the *News*, Cleveland's late afternoon papers, picked up her story the next day, followed by the city's morning paper, the *Plain Dealer*, on August 26. From then until the end of the month, the poignant story was headline news every day in both the *Press* and the *News*, and four out of six days in the ordinarily more restrained *Plain Dealer*.

Though neither the *News* nor the *Plain Dealer* remained exactly oblivious to the "human interest" angles that Beverly's disappearance offered, the *Press* pounced on the story with leonine ferocity and shook it unmercifully. Some of the paper's coverage reflected genuine concern—Ben Marino's articles remain particularly sensitive; but all too frequently, the *Press* responded to the tragedy with the same sort of Hearst-inspired, sledgehammer journalism it would employ three years later while covering Marilyn Sheppard's brutal murder—with excesses that would be a major factor in later overturning Sam Sheppard's original conviction, winning him a new trial and ultimately an acquittal. In a series of sensational front-page stories about Beverly that seemed designed to alternately terrify and pull at the heartstrings, the paper minutely examined every facet of the police investigation, reported on every single tip (no matter how trivial), kept its readers abreast of all the ongoing suffering in the Potts household, and issued a stream of dire warnings about all the dangers that lurked on city streets for unsuspecting youngsters. The paper also exhorted Clevelanders to cooperate fully with police in every way, keep their eyes opened for any clues, and be ever vigilant with their own children.

It would be tempting to argue that cynical local reporters, looking for something to write about during slow news days at the close of summer, latched on to the Potts case in such a way as to prove Orson Welles's famous contention in *Citizen Kane:* "If the headline is big enough, it makes the news big enough." But could a lack of news have been an issue at a time when the country was at war in Korea? Doris O'Donnell Beaufait, former reporter for both the *News* and the *Plain Dealer,* explains the city's single-minded fascination with the case in 1951 by recalling Tip O'Neill's famous quip: "All politics is local!"

The Beverly Potts mystery did not occur in a vacuum; there had been other incidents in the months leading up to her disappearance, some involving children, suggesting that at least part of the city's reaction may have been due to pent-up emotions and building anxiety. Three months before, in May, five-year-old Gail Ann Michel of Lakewood had been snatched and later abandoned in a downtown department store. In the same month, there were reports that two little girls had been "molested" in Halloran Park itself, and in the weeks before Beverly's disappearance, three different women had been the targets of what the *News* termed "sex attacks" in areas close to the Potts home. On the evening of New Year's Day, 1948, Harold Beach had stabbed eight-year-old Sheila Ann Tuley while she had been running an errand for her father. That brutal murder had occurred almost four years before, but the senseless slaying still reverberated in the city's memory to such an extent that comparisons with Beverly Potts, though there was never any solid proof at the time that she was murdered, were inevitable.

Part of the explanation for Beverly's enduring fascination may be a simple matter of time and place. In 1951 the area just south of Lorain and east of West 117 Street, from which she vanished, was a middle-class, *Leave-It-to-Beaver* neighborhood of neat, well-kept houses; it was a simpler, safer, *Father-Knows-Best* time, when residents left their doors unlocked and women could stroll down the streets after dark without worrying. It was inconceivable that a child could disappear so completely from such a well-ordered world, and when one did, that sense of neighborhood security was irrevocably shattered. "Things like that just didn't happen," asserts Donna J. Kensick, one of Beverly's classmates. Doris O'Donnell Beaufait remembers sitting on the front porch of the

The first day of classes at Louis Agassiz Elementary School in September 1951. Beverly had vanished a mere two weeks before this picture was taken. *Cleveland Press* Archives, Cleveland State University.

house almost directly across from the Potts residence in the company of the *Press*'s Ben Marino and other reporters, sipping lemonade and nibbling cookies (all provided by the accommodating housewives and mothers of Linnet Avenue) as she and her colleagues waited for an opportunity to interview Beverly's parents and neighbors. A homey, Betty-Crocker touch amidst the pain and uncertainty! "We never thought that she wouldn't be found," she reflected fifty years later. The serpent had entered the Garden of Eden.

Tragedy can bring out the best in people; it can also summon up the worst. The families of the Linnet Avenue neighborhood came to the Potts home bringing food and support; strangers phoned or stopped by to offer comfort and condolences. "Heart of a City Shows in Search for Missing Girl," proclaimed a *News* editorial on August 28. But cranks also called the house only to hang up or laugh menacingly; cruising motorists turned usually quiet Linnet Avenue into a major thoroughfare; and the morbidly curious gathered in such large numbers outside the Potts residence—simply to gawk at the house—that the police ultimately barricaded the street. Suddenly, an average, working-class family—its privacy snatched away and utterly destroyed—found itself floundering in the sort of intense media glare the prim and proper 1950s usually reserved for the scandalous behavior of Hollywood stars. Over time, dark whispers that not all was as it should be in the Potts household began to infect the atmosphere like poison gas rising from a swamp.

Such an inexplicable disappearance also inevitably affected Beverly's classmates, friends, and the children of the neighborhood—even those who were not acquainted with her. It was a "terrible thing," asserts classmate Donna Kensick. "Unheard of," insists neighbor Fred Krause. "We realized how horrible it was," Kensick reflects. "We kept hoping she would turn up." Today, the adult world responds to traumatic events involving children and teens—school shootings, automobile accidents, sudden deaths due to disease and the like—by making available a veritable army of grief counselors and psychologists. But in the 1950s, none of this existed. It was thought then that the best way to help children work through a tragedy was not to talk about it or even encourage them to express their feelings. Silence healed all psychic wounds.

If industrialist Cyrus Eaton is to be taken at his word, the Great Depression devastated Cleveland as no other major industrial center in the country. Though it remained the nation's sixth largest city, the 1940 census, for the first time in Cleveland history, documented a small decline in its population (878,336 as opposed to 900,429 in 1930), as residents with the money to do so began leaving the neighborhoods at the city's core and heading for the suburbs. The demand for war material, however, jolted the city out of its economic malaise and propelled industry into a period of rapid expansion to meet the need of the armed forces for everything from tanks to binoculars. In 1943 Mayor Frank J. Lausche organized the Postwar Planning Council to grapple, on the one hand, with the staggering problems of revitalizing what the Depression had destroyed and, on the other hand, to consolidate and build on the industrial advantages Cleveland had gained during the war. In 1944, noting that half the populations of both the United States and Canada lived within a five-hundred-mile radius, city fathers dubbed Cleveland "the best location in the nation"—the ideal geographic hub, with the necessary transportation systems for receiving and shipping the raw materials needed to keep industries flourishing. In the late 1940s, Mayor Thomas A. Burke spearheaded a successful drive to revitalize the downtown area. Only the start of the Korean War blighted the exuberant postwar optimism.

The combination of the Depression and World War II had put the brakes on the housing industry in the city proper and the suburbs, but postwar prosperity sparked greater demand for newer dwellings in Cleveland's outlying areas. Though wartime in-migration accounted for a 4.2 percent increase in the population by 1950, thousands of city residents were abandoning Cleveland's central neighborhoods for the suburbs as the result of progressive deterioration and rising crime.

The West Park neighborhood was one of the more stable in the city. The 12.5-square-mile area—bordered by West 117 Street to the east, Lakewood to the north, the Rocky River Valley to the west, and Brookpark Road to the south—had merged with Cleveland proper in 1923, the last of the old city suburbs to do so. In the late 1940s and early 1950s, the area just east of West 117 and south of Lorain Avenue reflected the stability of its neighbor to the west. Though today we tend to see the terms "middle class" and "working class" as almost mutually exclusive, fifty years ago both labels were used to describe the area just east of West Park—a neat, attractive, comfortable neighborhood where returning GIs and blue-collar workers, the children and grandchildren of European immigrants, began living out the promise of the American dream.

In 1945 the neighborhood jewel, Halloran Park, opened to the public. Situated between West 117 and West 120, the 11.5-acre expanse of fenced-in basketball courts, swings, monkey bars, teeter-totters, slides, and a baseball diamond (a swimming pool and an ice rink would be added later) served an estimated 100,000 area youngsters. The park immediately became a magnet for local children with time on their hands, especially during the lazy days of summer when school was out. Today, we would say it was a place for kids to hang out. "We just went to the park all the time—during the day—and just sat on the grass or the benches," recalls one of Beverly's classmates. Bordered on the north by Linnet Avenue and on the south by Cooley Avenue, the park was the only large playground in the area. In the early 1940s the land had been a dump, an untended open field covered with a tangle of weeds and refuse. The Cleveland Transit System, the owners of this urban eyesore, had originally intended to build housing for streetcars on the unused property, but in 1944 Cleveland's City Planning Commission won City Council's approval to buy the land for $28,500, with an additional allocation of

Halloran Park as it appeared in 1951, looking east toward West 117 Street and Linnet Avenue. *Cleveland Press* Archives, Cleveland State University.

$50,000 for cleanup, new trees, and playground equipment. In a flush of civic pride and patriotism, the park was named for William I. Halloran, a former local journalist employed by United Press International who went down with the *Arizona* when the Japanese bombed Pearl Harbor—the first Clevelander to die in World War II.

But from the beginning, something vaguely sinister hovered around the three-block-long park at night. Because it lacked interior lighting, Halloran was a dark, lonely place after the neighborhood children left it at the end of the day, and the sparseness of the newly planted young trees only added to the sense of naked emptiness. A half-dozen benches stood hidden in the shadows of the shelter at Halloran's north end, and local boys giggled secretively over the nightly "necking parties" there. The culvert through which Big Creek ran snaked from West 117 to West 130, looping north to cut through the lower end of the park; and the wild sprawl of woods and desolate, overgrown fields from which Halloran had been carved still encroached on its southern edge. Derelicts hung around on the playground's fringes; in the morning, empty wine bottles often turned up on some of the playing fields.

Beverly Potts's parents, Robert Potts and Elizabeth Treuer, both aged twenty-four years, were married on April 2, 1924, by Justice of the Peace J. E. Chizek. The Hungarian-born bride had been brought to the United States in 1904 at the age of four by her parents, Martin and Rozalia (nee Veros) Treuer. The family initially settled somewhere in the midst of the dirty, sprawling coal-mining communities of Pennsylvania, West Virginia, and Ohio. In the early years of the twentieth century, Cleveland could boast the largest Hungarian population in the world outside of Budapest, and it was, perhaps, a longing for the familiarity of the old country, coupled with the sheer size of its Hungarian colonies, that ultimately drew the Treuers to the city on the Erie shore. In those days, the city's largest Hungarian community, consisting primarily of blue-collar workers who found employment in the nearby factories, congregated on the East Side around East 117–120 streets in the Buckeye area, and it was on Cleveland's East Side that Joseph Treuer (Martin's son and Elizabeth's brother) settled sometime in 1915 or 1916. A smaller, more aristocratic Hungarian colony, however, gathered on the city's near West Side; so when Martin Treuer brought the rest of his family to Cleveland and joined his son a few years later in 1921, Joseph bought a multipurpose building containing at least two family units at 1966 West 52 Street. That building would remain in the Treuer family for the next fifty years. In the early 1920s, Elizabeth—possibly having adopted the stage name "Betty True"—worked as a vaudeville dancer at Luna Park, a thirty-five-acre amusement park on the city's East Side affectionately dubbed "Cleveland's fairyland of pleasure." It was at the park that she met the young stagehand who would become her husband in 1924.

The family history of Robert Potts—an average man of English, Scottish, and Irish decent with a common name—remains somewhat more obscure and difficult to trace. His forebears apparently lived in or around Columbus, Ohio, and Potts family roots reach back far enough in the United States to include a couple of Union Army Civil War veterans. The son of Robert Frank and Dency (nee Snellbacher or, perhaps, Snelbaker) Potts, he is simply identified on his 1924 marriage license as a laborer living at 1952 West 52 Street, obviously placing his residence very close to the Treuer household at 1966. The first sign of him in Cleveland occurs in 1921 when he and his father, Robert Sr., turn up on Carnegie Avenue. Though the city directory for 1924 does place the younger Potts at the West 52 Street address given on the license application, he was not there the year before nor the year after. In fact, both father and son seem to have escaped the notice of directory compilers until late 1927.

Both Elizabeth and Robert were of slight stature. In fact, since Robert measured only a shade over five feet in height, members of the family circle dubbed him "Little Pottsy"—as opposed to "Big Pottsy," his taller, older brother, William. (By the time she was twelve, the Pottses' first daughter, Anita, was taller than either of her parents, and evidence suggests that Beverly, had she lived, would have been taller as well.) Robert's tiny feet required shoes smaller than the smallest sizes made for adult males. Too stubborn—and, no doubt, too proud—to buy his footwear in the children's department, Robert indulged himself with custom-made shoes.

On April 4, 1929, five years after her marriage, Elizabeth Potts gave birth to her first child, Anita Lois Potts. Actress Anita Louise was a popular film star of the day, and Anita Potts occasionally found her middle name altered from Lois to Louise on official and semiofficial documents. In her eleventh year, Anita learned she was to become a big sister. "It was exciting at first," she recalls. "Later it was a lot of work," she adds with a hearty chuckle. Beverly Rose Potts was born at 7:34 P.M. on April 15, 1941. Society is likely to attach all sorts of labels to a baby girl born seventeen years into a marriage and twelve years after her nearest and only sibling: "a blessing," "a gift," "an afterthought," "a mistake," "a surprise." But Beverly Potts was truly a "miracle child." Born two months premature at only three pounds, two ounces, the tiny, fragile infant spent the first weeks of her life in an incubator. Beverly was so small and so pink, her mother affectionately nicknamed her Rosebud.

On September 10, 1927, Robert—now a stagehand at the Riverside Theater near Kamm's Corners—and Elizabeth bought a house at 11304 Linnet Avenue, a neat, attractive street south of Lorain Avenue and just off West 117 Street. Like many of the streets in all older city neighborhoods, Linnet was and is rather narrow by contemporary standards, and a modern suburbanite who prizes his elbow room would find the smallish houses too close to the street and too close to each other for comfort. (It remains something of a mystery where the newlyweds were living during the three years immediately following their marriage. It is not only possible but likely that the bride's parents temporarily shared

Rosebud blossoming. Beverly at about fifteen months. Elizabeth Potts wrote "The little immigrant" on the back of this picture. Courtesy of Anita Potts Georges.

their home on West 52nd with the young couple, perhaps, even with Robert's father as well.) The house on Linnet was listed in Elizabeth's name from the time of its purchase until her death in 1956. Though today such a creative dodge would be impossible, it was a common ploy in the years leading up to and including the Great Depression to list a house in the wife's name, so that if the husband fell into debt, creditors could not touch the family home. In this instance, Robert also apparently felt that his leadership position on the executive board of the Stagehands Union, AFL Local 27, could make him an attractive target for lawsuits. Economically, it was touch-and-go for the new, struggling family for several years, and at one point the couple would have lost their house had it not been for the financial intervention of Elizabeth's parents. During the years of the Great Depression, Robert and Elizabeth made room in their small home for a host of relatives on both sides of the family. "We had an endless stream of people living with us," Anita recalls. "My father's brother and his wife moved in when I was very small, but I remember them being there. My mother's parents, my grandmother and grandfather [Rozalia and Martin Treuer], lived with us. In

The former Potts home at 11304 Linnet Avenue as it appears today. Photo by Denise Blanda.

fact, my grandmother delivered me because the doctor didn't believe I was on the way." For the Potts family, the move to 11304 Linnet Avenue was a step upward economically and, perhaps, socially, and they were still living in the quaint, cottage-like house twenty-four years later when their younger daughter vanished.

When I began exploring the disappearance of Beverly Potts in the spring of 2002, I naively assumed that the entire research process would move forward far more swiftly and easily than it had when I was digging into the history of the Kingsbury Run murders. After all, she had vanished during my lifetime; the Butcher had dispatched and dismembered his victims before I was born. The mere fifteen-year gap that separated the two crimes seemed an eternity—the difference between ancient and modern history. I soon discovered, however, that newspaper accounts from the early 1950s remained just as prone to bits of misinformation, discrepancies, and omissions as their counterparts from the mid-1930s; and though police records could often correct or clarify details reported by the press, they presented their own special problems. The collection of surviving official reports on the Potts case in the homicide unit of the Cleveland Police Department contains material from 1951 to 2002 and is massive enough to fill a rather large box, but this original documentation remains sufficiently incomplete and disorganized that it is impossible to derive any coherent, overall picture of official actions from reading through it. The legions of foot soldiers involved in the search for Beverly Potts were each rather like the proverbial blind man with the elephant: individuals only knew that part of the case that they touched personally. James McArthur, who headed up the investigation, and David Kerr, head of homicide, were the only authorities involved who could command an overall view of the entire campaign. A bundle of directives from McArthur's office tucked among the reports clearly demonstrates the degree to which he was in charge and how familiar he was with every detail of the investigation. The files, however, are obviously incomplete, and Kerr may be at least partly responsible for the gaps in the official documentation. In 2001 Detective Robert Wolf interviewed the one-time chief of homicide repeatedly about the Beverly Potts case. Then in his early 90s and living in a Vermillion, Ohio, nursing home, Kerr admitted he had taken police files from Cleveland's most famous cases—the Sheppard murder, the Kingsbury Run killings, and the disappearance of Beverly Potts—with him when he retired in 1972 because he intended to write a book. (That book never materialized, and the fate of those purloined documents remains a mystery.) Still, to read through the Potts files is to fully understand that police work in the real world is not *Law and Order* or *NYPD Blue*. Every lead, no matter how trivial it seemed, had to be thoroughly checked and reported upon in numbing detail; and all this official attention to the minutiae of the case occurred in the days before computers.

Newspapers are not—nor were they ever intended to be—history; they are vehicles for the quick transmission of information—entities with a twenty-four-hour lifespan to be consumed, tossed away, and replaced by their successors the next day. In such a high-profile case, city papers seized on every shred of information; every potential lead and every official action, no matter how insignificant, found its way into the pages of Cleveland's dailies. But unless those reports led to something newsworthy, those threads of information were never picked up again. Also, a newspaper's primary focus remains "the big picture"

(Beverly Potts is missing! The police have mounted an all-out search! The Potts family is in agony!), but the devil is in the details. Though any reputable paper strives for accuracy, the rush to meet publication deadlines and beat the competition inevitably creates an environment in which errors of all sorts flourish. In the few days immediately following Beverly's disappearance, the stories from Cleveland's three daily papers perpetrate a variety of discrepancies, some significant, some trivial: confusions as to the time element, disagreements as to whether individuals acted alone or in concert, differences as to who saw or did what and when, conflicting accounts as to whether those involved in the search walked the streets or drove a car, differing reports as to whether Elizabeth Potts took a sedative or not during the first days of the hunt for her daughter. And Elizabeth Potts's age fluctuates between forty-nine and fifty-one. There's even a disagreement over the state of Beverly's hair; was it her mother or Beverly herself who had decided her long pigtails should be shorn in favor of bangs?

Given the size and energy of the investigation, the parade of potential suspects, especially viable ones, remains astonishingly short. Newspapers generally identified a suspect by age—sometimes by street of residence or profession—but never by name. Consequently, when reports about a particular suspect are carried from one story to the next or pass from one paper to a competitor, it is often difficult—at times impossible—to be certain who is being referred to. (If the police reports dealing with the same incident are available, then it is possible to give an otherwise unidentified suspect a name.) These are small points, perhaps, especially given the seriousness and poignancy of "the big picture." But writing history means nailing down all those specifics, and in this case, that proved at least as difficult as straightening out the details surrounding the Kingsbury Run murders. A Gordian knot is a Gordian knot.

In the first chapters of this book, I try to present a simple chronology of the events that began in the evening of August 24, 1951, when Beverly disappeared, and that continued through the first weeks of the hunt; but constructing that sequence proved anything but simple. When the *Plain Dealer* reported on the investigation, I assumed those events had taken place the day before. I similarly assumed that anything covered by the *Press* or the *News*, the city's afternoon-evening papers, probably happened either the day before or, possibly, earlier the same day; but often it was not clear exactly where in the timeline a particular piece of the ongoing story belonged. The use of such signifiers as "yesterday" or "last night" was helpful, but the frequent use of such vague terms as "earlier" only compounded the problem. How much earlier? The same day? The day before? Or, perhaps, even "earlier"? The papers would also report on a number of investigative initiatives within a single story without clarifying whether these events occurred one after the other or happened simultaneously.

When a newspaper story quoted an investigator, a witness, a member of the Potts family, or a neighbor directly, I assumed that the individual in question was being quoted with at least reasonable accuracy— that those words were taken down by a reporter who either interviewed face to face the person to whom the quote was being attributed or was present when the statement was made. I made the same assumption whenever a reporter paraphrased a source but identified that individual by name. Other elements of the contemporary newspaper coverage were, however, considerably more problematic. The game of one-upmanship among Cleveland's competing dailies dictated that at times reporters repeat rumors, leads, tips, or other bits of information that came to them second-, third-, or fourth-hand. Some of the details provided, therefore, are either—at worst—untrustworthy or—at best—extremely vague. Also, what seems to be two different leads or separate incidents may, in fact, actually be the same thing repeated in garbled form. Is one person's late-model car, menacingly cruising the neighborhood, the same vehicle as another witness's late-model car?

In some obvious respects, the police reports represent a vast improvement over the newspaper coverage. They are far longer, much more detailed and precise, and—for the most part—free from any sort of editorial commentary. Regrettably, however, they are not error-free. A witness's account does not suddenly become more accurate simply because he or she is talking to a policeman rather than a reporter, and the official documentation perpetuates its own set of errors and embraces all sorts of contradictions. The name of Elizabeth Potts's cousin Betty Morbito is spelled a number of different ways in police reports, and Beverly's sister, Anita, is called "Juanita" in one document. Police reports also drop a given line of investigation without comment if a lead fails to pan out, thus leaving students of the case dangling without resolution.

Since it has only been fifty years since Beverly Potts vanished, many of her classmates and friends, now in their early sixties, should still be around. But in the half century since that fateful August night, many have married (a major problem when trying to trace women), moved, or otherwise disappeared. One woman was far more interested in talking about how I managed to track her down than she was in sharing her memories of Beverly Potts.

Over the last few years the American public has been bludgeoned repeatedly with heartbreaking stories of child abduction and murder. In each case, the familiar, often tragic, chain of events inevitably followed: the determined search and the agonized wait, the gathering of worried friends and relatives offering what comfort they can, the heartrending public appeals from the parents for their child's safe return. The disappearance of Beverly Potts marked, perhaps, one of the first times that this somber ritual—both reported on and driven by the media—played itself out in such an intense glare of public scrutiny. In one vital respect, however, the Beverly Potts disappearance is different from all others. Generally, public awareness in such cases fades as media attention dwindles and hopes for a safe return die; renewed interest erupts only if a perpetrator is captured, a body discovered, or—as in the case of Elizabeth Smart—the abducted child is returned alive. Hope for Beverly Potts seemingly died more than a half century ago. No perpetrator was ever charged or even identified in her disappearance. It remains a haunting enigma without closure, and yet, at least in Cleveland, the memory of her endures. She has become the symbol for all missing children. But fifty years after her disappearance, she remains a legend with a forgotten history, a face with a forgotten story. And the poignant tragedy of Beverly Potts is not just the story of a missing child; it is the tale of unbearable family grief, of intense public reaction both kind and cruel, of massive police response (on both the departmental and individual levels), of unprecedented, invasive media scrutiny, and, ultimately, of the circumstances that converge to create a legend.

It is also a story that took hold of me at a time when one of the last things I wanted to think about was starting another book about an unsolved crime. And the reason that I was so vulnerable is utterly simple: I have a debt to pay. Like all youngsters, my mother had drilled me until I could recite my name, address, and telephone number without thinking. I still have a fleeting image of her standing in front of me while I dutifully and uncomprehendingly ran through the litany: "My name is Jimmy Badal, and I live at 18000 Winslow Road, and my phone number is LO 3977." Naturally, I also had gotten the dire warnings about strangers and their cars. I learned my lessons well. On a late summer after-

The Potts family at Christmas 1947, when Beverly was six. From left to right: Anita; Elizabeth; Beverly; the family dog, Center Door Fancy (a stage term— Fancy for short); and Robert. Though reportedly shy, Beverly obviously plays to the camera, clearly having inherited her mother's flare for the stage. Courtesy of Anita Potts Georges.

noon, while standing at the end of the block on the quiet Shaker Heights street where I lived, a dark-colored car with two men in it pulled quickly up to the curb. The man on the passenger side stuck his head menacingly and deliberately through the open window: "Do you want to go for a ride?" Like a vague memory from an old dream, the image blurs and fades when I try to look at it closely. Only the man's face, no doubt demonized over the years, remains clear—dark, craggy, unshaven, and partially obscured by his hat. "No," I can still hear myself answering timidly before running home.

Beverly Potts was my senior by two years. Born in 1941, she vanished ten years later in 1951, when I would have been eight. In recent years, I've wrestled with the notion that I may have escaped kidnapping the same summer she disappeared. Somehow, though, I see myself as younger than eight when this attempted abduction occurred, but I can't be sure. All I know is I ran home and to safety on an auburn afternoon more than fifty years ago with my light summer jacket flapping behind me. Jimmy Badal was lucky; Beverly Potts was not.

NOTES

The statistics relevant to the city's economic and social situations in the years between the Depression and the postwar period are recorded in *The Encyclopedia of Cleveland History,* edited by David D. Van Tassel and John J. Grabowski. The details of Halloran Park's history are taken from an August 20, 1951, article in the *Press.*

Anita Potts supplied most of the background information on her parents and her younger sister, Beverly. The marriage of Robert Potts and Elizabeth Treuer is recorded on license application no. 189202. That document, I should note, contains a couple of errors. The name of Robert's mother, Dency Snellbacher, is given as Denise Snellbecker, and through some sort of inexplicable bureaucratic magic, the name of Elizabeth's mother is metamorphosed from Rozalia Veros to Rose Roth. Again, I am indebted to Anita Potts for straightening out the tangle of errors.

PART ONE

Dusk and Shadow

A Very Ordinary Day

The earth might as well have opened up and swallowed the child.
She has vanished into nothing.
Ben R. Tidyman in the Plain Dealer, *September 4, 1951*

Within hours of the decision, it would become one that Elizabeth Potts desperately wished she could take back, one that would haunt and torment her until the day she died, a mere five years later in 1956. Her daughter Beverly had finagled a major concession from her; she could go to nearby Halloran Park that evening with her next-door neighbor and best friend, Patricia (Patsy) Swing, to see the show. The day before, Elizabeth Potts had forbidden her usually obedient ten-year-old to go to the park for two weeks because the child had lost track of time while playing there with her cousin, six-year-old Amber Lathan, but this was special: as a fond farewell to the last days of summer before children returned to school, the City Recreation Department and the *Cleveland Press,* one of the city's two afternoon newspapers, were jointly sponsoring a Showagon—a now virtually forgotten form of neighborhood entertainment featuring strictly local talent in a series of vaudeville-like acts that made the rounds of recreation centers in a combination truck and traveling stage.

And it certainly did not seem that by relenting on her strictures of the previous day Elizabeth Potts was "giving in" or in any way encouraging rebellious behavior in her younger daughter. Everyone who knew Beverly agreed that she was obedient, polite, and shy. The only reported source of ongoing conflict between mother and daughter involved Beverly's inability to keep track of time and be home when she was told.

(On the day before—Thursday, August 23—Elizabeth had spanked her with a ruler because Amber and Beverly had missed a curfew on two separate occasions on the same day.) Though she was only ten years old, neighbors—as well as her parents—deemed her sufficiently responsible to babysit their very young children. (Two-and-a-half-year-old Robert Bassak and three-year-old Cheryl Koch, both of Linnet Avenue, were among her charges.) In fact, Beverly seems to have been particularly fond and protective of children younger than she. One Linnet Avenue resident later remembered that Beverly had walked her daughter to kindergarten every day for the first few weeks of school. Norma Mazey, Beverly's fourth-grade teacher at Louis Agassiz Elementary School on Bosworth Road, couldn't remember ever having to discipline the strikingly attractive child; she was "a model pupil" she told the *Cleveland News* on August 29—a B student, shy perhaps, but certainly not backward, who got along well with her classmates, both girls and boys. Patsy Swing later recalled that the only boy that Beverly had "liked" was classmate Robert Bloor. (Her shyness, in fact, especially around men and boys, would later become a major issue in the investigation.) As the daughter of a former vaudeville performer, Beverly dearly loved music and dancing; she was truly her mother's child. She played the cello in the school orchestra, and the sight of her daughter wrestling with an instrument case as large as she remained a constant source of amusement for Elizabeth Potts. For months, Beverly had unsuccessfully lobbied her mother to cut her long, blond pigtails so she could wear her hair in bangs—a tangible sign that she was growing up. Finally in June, Elizabeth Potts relented. She clipped her daughter's braids, complete with the green ribbons coiled around them, and lovingly packed them away in tissue paper.

For Beverly, the Friday evening entertainment at Halloran would be only the first item on a very full weekend itinerary. The next day, according to press reports, the entire Potts family had planned an all-day outing and picnic at Euclid Beach Park; Beverly had even turned down a party invitation in anticipation of such an exciting, major excursion.

The record is cloudy on this point. Although all contemporary sources seem to agree that the Potts family planned to go to Euclid Beach on Saturday, August 25, Beverly's older sister, Anita, who was in her early twenties at the time, disputes this. She points out that the amusement park on the east side of Cuyahoga County would have been too far away for a family living off of West 117 Street and further insists that her father's erratic work schedule as a stagehand at the Allen Theater would have made any kind of family plans of that sort difficult. Though she does not remember any specific plans for a family outing the next day, Anita asserts that Puritas Springs Park, overlooking the Rocky River Valley, would have been a much more likely destination. Two separate police reports, however, specifically refer to the planned excursion—one dated August 31, 1951, the other September 4. The latter of these reports states that Betty Morbito—Elizabeth Potts's cousin then living with the Potts family—planned to drive Beverly to the East Side amusement park. Since the official document fails to mention any other members of the Potts family, it seems reasonable to assume that the outing involved only Beverly and this cousin.

That evening, however, members of the Potts household—Beverly's parents Robert and Elizabeth, her sister, Anita, and Betty Morbito—were consumed by affairs more adult than picnics, playground shows, and park outings. In a tight American League pennant race, Cleveland held a few games' lead over New York, and the Tribe was taking on the hated Yankees at Lakefront Stadium that night. The day before, pitching ace Bob Lemon had hurled the hometown boys to a 2 to 1 victory over New York's finest; that night Early Wynn, already with fourteen wins behind him, would be taking the mound for the good guys. Newspapers estimated that seventy thousand screaming Clevelanders would turn up at the stadium that evening of August 24. Every baseball fan on Linnet Avenue would be glued to his TV or radio.

The Potts family finished dinner sometime between 6:30 and 6:45. There was a slight nip in the air that night, so Beverly slipped a blue jacket over her reddish-pink turtleneck shirt and blue denim jeans. She had earned a nickel for helping her mother with the supper dishes, but she did not take her wages with her when she and Patsy Swing headed for the park on their bicycles—though Halloran was only a five- to seven-minute walk away—close to 7:00. Lester Swing and his family had moved next door to the Potts home at 11304 Linnet Avenue from Lockport, New York, in 1944, when Beverly had been three and Patsy four, and the two girls had been best friends ever since, in spite of the usual childhood squabbles. They were together constantly, playing in either the Potts or the Swing house. "Patsy was in the house all the time or else Beverly went to her house," Anita recalls. "She [Patsy] seemed to me about the same as Beverly—fairly quiet." The day before, the two girls had played with Beverly's dolls and dollhouse on the Pottses' front porch, along

Very best friends. Patsy Swing and Beverly in the late 1940s. Though
a year younger and a year behind Patsy in school, Beverly was already
tall for her age. Courtesy of Anita Potts Georges.

with friend Karen Kilbane. Except for those weekends when the Potts
family went visiting, they would go to the matinee together every Saturday at the Variety Theater on Lorain Avenue, close to West 117. "We
liked funny pictures, not cowboy shows," Patsy recalled to *Cleveland
News* reporter Doris O'Donnell Beaufait on Tuesday, August 28.

Cleveland has always manifested a combination of the cosmopolitan
and the parochial: elements of the big city and the small town combined, a mixture perplexing to outsiders and a source of both pride and
embarrassment to locals. Although the crowd that gathered in Halloran

Park that night for the show was later estimated to number about fifteen hundred people, the atmosphere remained surprisingly intimate: a rural village celebration in the midst of a major metropolis. The two youngsters didn't talk with anyone once they arrived; surprisingly, Patsy later reported that they saw no one they knew, though the crowd, in spite of its size, surely must have included neighbors, friends, and classmates. (Thirteen-year-old Carol Katrenick of Dale Avenue and her friend Lillian Szymanski, however, later remembered running into the two girls and greeting them with a brief "hello.") But at ninety pounds and four feet, eleven inches in height, Beverly was a shade tall for her ten years, and at least a few park visitors saw her that night as she and Patsy wandered among the gathering spectators. "I don't remember what she was doing or whom she was with, but I saw her," reflects classmate Donna Kensick fifty years later.

Their bicycles quickly became major impediments. With so many people at Halloran, riding them in the playground itself was obviously out of the question, and—with no safe or convenient place to park them—walking with them through such a large milling crowd proved difficult. When the show began at 8:00, the situation became impossible. There was no way they could keep an eye on their bikes and watch the proceedings on stage at the same time, so at approximately 8:10, the two girls decided to take their bikes home, leave them in their respective garages, and return to the park on foot. That evening, the sun went down at 8:16 P.M., just as Patsy and Beverly pedaled down the street and swung into their driveways. Margaret Swing called for her daughter to come into the house, but Patsy protested that Beverly's mother was allowing her to return to the show. Mrs. Swing relented and let Patsy go with her—as long as she returned before dark. The girls arrived back at Halloran sometime before 8:30. As dark shadows stretched slowly and relentlessly across the park, ominous—though fleeting—undercurrents ran silently below the surface gaiety and anticipation of the large crowd. Some children watched, their interest tinged with alarm, as an older man in need of a shave cruised slowly around the playground in a dark car, later described by some of those who saw it as a 1937 or 1938 black Dodge coupe. While the show was still going on, the driver pulled his car into the park area. "It was so close to me I rubbed a red smudge off the rear trunk," an unidentified boy told the *News*. (A police report dated August 27 documents the incident—or one very much like it—and identifies the driver as Louis Schisller.) Around 8:30 Cleveland Police patrolman George Vorell, off duty and

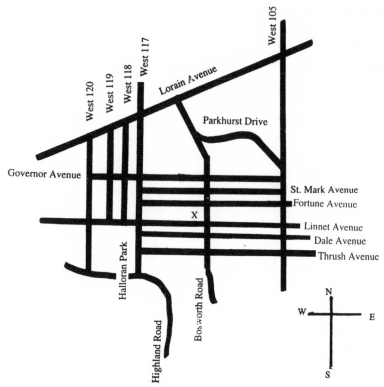

The Halloran Park—Linnet Avenue neighborhood. The Showagon was positioned on the left side of the park, midway between the north and south ends. In 1951 a paved walk led diagonally from the center of Halloran to the West 117–Linnet Avenue intersection. After the show ended, newsboy and neighbor Fred Krause was riding his bicycle in a northeast direction, on the grass and to the right of the walkway, when he passed someone he later identified as possibly being Beverly Potts. The Potts family residence (x) at 11304 Linnet is on the north side of the street, a few houses west of Bosworth Road. The house is no more than a five-minute stroll from Halloran Park.

attending the show with his young son, watched suspiciously as two young men between the ages of seventeen and twenty—one blond, the other sporting dark, wavy hair—prowled around the Showagon, seemingly checking out very young girls. The pair eventually wandered behind the stage and disappeared. Patricia Nagg, a friend of Beverly's, watched uneasily at the odd manner in which a thin man in his twenties applauded the acts on stage; as he brought his hands together, he thrust his hips forward and backward in movements that suggested copulation.

Fathers held children perched on their shoulders, and the sheer size of the crowd made it difficult for the two girls to see what was going on. Part of the area in front of the stage had been roped off and reserved for younger children, but Beverly and Patsy had to stand on tiptoe and crane their necks to get a glimpse of the performers on the makeshift stage set on an incline near the shelter house. Thirteen-year-old Fred Krause of 11500 Linnet Avenue was riding his bicycle at the northwestern end of the park, looking for someone he knew, and he saw Beverly and Patsy standing at one end of the Showagon. At 8:30 P.M., as the evening darkened, Fred Krause's mother, Dorothy, stepped out on the front lawn of the family house and watched for her son and husband to return. The elder Krause had gone off somewhere to buy a part for the TV set, and Fred was apparently still peddling around Halloran Park. The family residence stood seven houses down from the corner on the north side of the street, thus assuring Mrs. Krause a clear view of both the West 117–Linnet intersection and the north end of the park.

Patsy Swing found it all rather uninteresting, and at 8:45, as darkness slowly began to settle, she turned to Beverly and suggested they had better go home. "My mother said I should be home before dark," she explained. But Beverly was entranced, especially by the singers and dancers; she told her friend that her mother had said it would be all right for her to stay through the entire show and that she would follow along in a few minutes. "I told her she had better come along with me," Patsy told the *Press* on August 25, but Beverly insisted on staying. So Patsy left. She turned once and looked back at her friend as she walked away. Later she could not remember if Beverly had even said, "So long!" "Her mother told her to be home by 9:00, and she was," reflects Anita Potts fifty years later. "My mother always loved music and watching the variety shows on TV or at the theaters—those big musical productions. And Beverly had that love of watching people dance and making music," she told Mark Wade Stone of Cleveland-based documentary filmmakers Storytellers Media Group in November 2003. "So she had gotten permission from my mother to stay to the end of the show. Although I'm sure my mother wasn't aware that Patsy Swing had been told to be home by 9:00 P.M." Patsy peered in the window of Walter's Bar on the southeast corner of West 117 and Linnet to check the time and then turned east on to Linnet Avenue and walked slowly to her home at 11308, all the while nursing a mild flush of resentment that Beverly had not come with her. She looked up and caught sight of Mr. and Mrs. Martin Pilot of

Patsy Swing as photo-
graphed by the *Press* in the
days immediately follow-
ing Beverly's disappear-
ance. The picture is one of
several taken by the paper
of Beverly's next-door
neighbor and best friend.
This shot is one of the
more flattering of the series, though the smile on
Patsy's face clearly masks
the painful inner turmoil
with which she was trying
to cope. *Cleveland Press* Archives, Cleveland State
University.

11416 Linnet, parents of her friend Marilyn, walking west toward the
park. When she arrived home at 8:50—she told the *Press* on August 28
that, for reasons she could not explain, she checked the time—she vented
her hurt feelings to her father. All was not always rosy between the two
best friends. According to Patsy, Beverly had a temper and could not
take a joke well. There had even been an incident two weeks before
when Beverly had slapped her over a "hidden" undershirt. "But we always made up," Patsy assured the *News* on August 28. "She and Beverly
would get into spats sometimes," Anita confirmed recently, "and they'd
both raise their voices."

Darkness closed in quickly on Linnet Avenue in late August. At the
height of summer, when the foliage of the maple and chestnut trees
lining the street was at its fullest, light from the streetlights barely made
it to the sidewalk. There were only four lights on Linnet, and they
twinkled like distant stars amidst the shifting dark clouds of leaves. Black

shadows loomed everywhere; the lingering breezes whispered through the trees. "This is the poorest lighted street in the city when the trees are all out," complained Beverly's father bitterly to the *Press* on August 28. More than a half century later, Anita concurred. "And they [the trees] were so huge that the light from the streetlights didn't penetrate the leaves. So unless you were right under the light pole, you couldn't see any light. It was pitch dark between lights walking on the sidewalk." The slight nip in the air had settled into a chill that Friday night, one just sharp enough to keep those few residents not watching or listening to the baseball game off their front porches. From West 117, Linnet Avenue stretched to the east: dark, lonely, quiet, deserted. At the same time that Patsy Swing wandered slowly home alone, shortly before 9:00, Robert Karmecy, a part-time Yellow Cab driver, picked up at West 117 and Detroit a "Polish-looking" man between twenty-five and thirty years old with a tallish, young girl sporting bangs who appeared to be about eleven years old and drove the pair to the bus station at East 13 and Chester Avenue.

At close to 9:30, Mary Hunt of 11012 Linnet Avenue became concerned about her three grandsons, Robert (twelve), Carl (eleven), and Henry (eight), so she strolled down the road toward Halloran, arriving just in time to catch the last two acts. She saw no one on the street. When the performances ended, apparently between 9:30 and 9:45, the lights that had illuminated the platform stage were turned off, casting a heavy, black veil of darkness over the entire playground; the crowd began to disperse quickly, breaking into smaller groups and heading off in different directions. Fred Krause's mother, still standing in front of the family home at 11500 Linnet Avenue, heard the voice over the loudspeaker announce that the show was over. Mary Hunt headed home, only to find her three missing grandsons parked happily in front of the family TV. A police cruiser had pulled silently into the park about the time proceedings on the stage were winding down, and the men inside watched as the attendees wandered away but saw nothing unusual. The police car waited until the performers had packed up and were ready to leave—perhaps as late as 10:20—and then drove off. Fourteen-year-old Gloria Vrana of 11512 Linnet Avenue and her twelve-year-old friend Patricia Kovar of West 117 strolled east across the park. The pair hung around the water fountain for a short time and then walked down Linnet to Gloria's house, where they took up residence on the Vrana front porch around 10:00. Fred Krause, still cruising around the park on his bicycle, had to ride on the lawn because of the large number of people strolling home on the sidewalks. He had to be careful; with all the interior lighting turned off, Halloran was almost pitch black. The large crowd rolled silently across the darkened landscape like a huge, black wave toward the streetlights on Linnet and West 117.

As he headed diagonally across the playground in a northeast direction toward his Linnet Avenue home, Fred noticed a dark form directly in front of him, somewhat detached from the main mass of the homebound crowd, walking on the grass just to the right of the walkway, heading toward the intersection of West 117 and Linnet. Even in the dark and from behind, something about the silhouette struck him as familiar; it was the curious and distinctive way the shape walked—something like a duck. As the boy pedaled closer, he identified the shadowed form as a young girl, and he wondered absentmindedly where he had seen that walk before. After all, he was the local delivery boy for the *Press,* and he knew most of the people in the neighborhood, at least by sight. Fleetingly, it occurred to Fred that he had seen the girl earlier in the evening somewhere else, with someone else; but now she was entirely alone. He tooted the horn on the handlebars of his bicycle as he passed by, giving the vaguely familiar girl only the most casual glance; and then he glided on, leaving her behind. Intent on getting home, the boy raised himself from his bicycle seat like a champion jockey and raced to the intersection, beating the great mass of the departing crowd. He then took his victory lap east on Linnet Avenue to his home seven houses down from the corner, parked his bicycle in the garage, and joined his mother and the family dog on the front lawn, where they remained—according to one police report—until 10:30. More than a week later, Fred Krause would wonder about that girl who walked like a duck. "I was in the living room with my mother," he recalled recently, "and I remember telling her, 'I might have seen her [Beverly Potts].'"

Other park visitors saw Beverly, or thought they saw her, at Halloran that Friday night; most eyewitness accounts placed her there from between 9:15 and 9:30, one as late as 10:00. Although she later retracted her story, nine-year-old Marlene Kloos of Peelor Avenue told police she had attended the show with her older sister, and as the two headed home, she noticed a green car, containing two young men, parked on Linnet Avenue facing east, the direction Beverly would have had to walk as she went home. Marlene knew Beverly, at least by sight, from Louis Agassiz Elementary School, and as she watched the parked car, she thought she saw someone who looked like Beverly get into it. A number of people noticed someone who looked like Beverly standing beside what the newspapers later described as a 1937 black Dodge coupe—distinguished by its smoking, noisy muffler, crude paint job, and recently repaired fenders—and talking to the two men inside. One had blond hair, the other dark brown or black. One witness put their ages at seventeen or eighteen, others in the early twenties. Thirteen-year-old Carol Katrenick had actually seen the car a couple of times during the evening. At about 8:45, she had glanced toward the West 117–Linnet Avenue intersection and noticed Patsy Swing heading home. She later insisted to the police that Beverly had suddenly run up to her departing friend and exchanged a few words with her (an assertion Patsy Swing would later firmly reject), walked over to the idling automobile, and bent over to talk with the two men inside. (Since, by all accounts, there were two young men in this 1937 black Dodge coupe, it clearly was not the same vehicle that several youngsters saw earlier in the evening being driven by a single older man.

Linnet Avenue as it appears today looking west toward Halloran Park and West 117 Street. The former Potts residence is on the north side. Many of the large trees that lined the narrow neighborhood street in 1951 and obscured the light from the street lights were felled by storms in the 1960s. The lighting on the street is far better now than it was in 1951 when Beverly disappeared. Photo by Denise Blanda.

The various descriptions, however, make the pair inside sound remark-ably similar to the two young men who had aroused Vorell's suspicious attention around 8:30.) Different reports of the encounter placed the car either on the east or west side of West 117 and put the incident anywhere from 8:30—fifteen minutes or so before Patsy Swing even left the park—to 9:30. But on one point everyone agreed; no one saw the girl they all thought might be Beverly get into the mysterious black car.

The August 29 issue of the *Plain Dealer* reported that a young girl, an out-of-town visitor, saw Beverly "swinging on the door handles of a convertible automobile parked near-by on the park's lawn." Could this "convertible" be the same car as the 1937 Dodge? The witness, who was about Beverly's age, saw two men enter the car, but insisted the girl she thought might be Beverly did not get in with them. She placed the curi-ous incident at about 10:00, a full half hour later than any of the other reported sightings. Mrs. Dorothy McCoy of Dale Avenue indirectly con-tradicted the girl's story, at least her estimation as to the time this event supposedly took place. In an eerie set of circumstances that prefigured the tragic events to come, Mrs. McCoy had watched the performances with her five-year-old son, Garry. Somehow, the youngster had slipped away around the time the show ended, and in her desperate search for her child, the frantic mother had returned to Halloran alone somewhere between 10:00 and 10:15, only to find the park dark and deserted. Her story had a happy ending; her missing son turned up asleep on the front porch of their Dale Avenue home. Mrs. McCoy later told police she was the last person to leave Halloran Park, and she had seen nothing out of the ordinary. At 9:45, an unidentified woman at West 110 and Baltic Avenue watched curiously as a dark 1948 coupe, driven by a forty-some-year-old man, sped north on Baltic. Three times she thought she heard the desperate cry, "I want to get out!" To her shocked disbelief, she later reported, she saw a young girl, her hands seemingly tied down behind her, thrashing in the back seat. At almost the exact moment, Edna We-ber stood outside her store at 7993 Lorain watching a Showagon truck heading east. A small, young girl sat on the passenger side, her eyes staring back down Lorain to the west. At 10:15, Mrs. Ida Steep visited the ladies' room at the Lyric Theater on Lorain Avenue, only to be con-fronted by three very young girls with cigarettes—one of whom she was sure was Beverly Potts. (She later remembered the incident because it struck her at the time that all three were far too young to be smoking.) At 10:30, Patricia Kovar's mother closed down the gas station she ran at

S. OH 6/28

Lanier, Shannon M

the northwest corner of Linnet and West 117, walked over into the deserted park, and looked around. She saw nothing.

It was close to 10:00 in the evening. Darkness had long since settled in completely, but Beverly had not returned home. Her parents, Robert and Elizabeth Potts, and her sister, Anita, began to worry. Occasionally, they stared out of the house's front windows up the quiet, dark street toward West 117, but there was no sign of the child. Perhaps she had come back with Patsy Swing and was still playing next door. At close to 10:00, her sense of apprehension growing, Anita Potts phoned the Swing family. A few moments later, she slowly returned the receiver to its cradle and told her parents that Patsy had returned more than an hour earlier; Beverly had not come back with her. "So we all went out on the porch and looked around," reflects Anita. "There was not a soul walking around." Robert Potts and Anita then left the house and walked hurriedly and silently up Linnet Avenue to see if Beverly had lingered at Halloran Park for some reason. But what could that reason be? What could possibly keep her there after dark, after the show, after everyone else had left? Coincidently, August 24 also marked the last day of the official park season; that same day, playground crews had taken an inventory of park equipment, removed the swings, and locked the shelter house. Even if Beverly had remained at the park, what was there for her to do? She had even planned to be in bed early that night in anticipation of the reported Euclid Beach outing on Saturday. Beverly's anxious father and sister walked hurriedly down the street. Linnet Avenue stretched before them dark and deserted; there was no one. The neat, small houses glided by like mute sentinels as the pair hurried toward the park. West 117 was and is a major, well-traveled city artery. Anita and her father stood silently on the corner watching the headlights cut through the darkness as cars sped by. Across the busy street, Halloran Park stretched into the nighttime gloom, as empty and forbidding as a desert, its earlier crowd of a thousand or more local residents dispersed; now it was quiet. And there was no sign of Beverly.

Sometime after 10:00, their worry surely swelling into full-blown panic, Anita and Robert Potts took the same lonely walk up Linnet Avenue that Patsy Swing had taken an hour before. Father and daughter would make a second, desperate visit to Halloran Park later that night. Perhaps Beverly was there; perhaps, somehow, they had missed her earlier. (Again, there are conflicting reports at this point. According to contemporary accounts, the Potts family only checked Halloran Park once, and there are conflicting versions as to whether Anita went alone or in the company of her father. Similarly, city papers relate that Robert Potts either walked or drove through the neighborhood searching for his daughter before authorities were called, but Anita insists they went directly home after the second visit to Halloran.) According to case records, Elizabeth Potts called police and reported her daughter missing at 10:57 P.M.

About midnight or shortly thereafter, George R. Hess of Parma, Ohio, sat in his car at the Lorain Avenue–West 117 intersection, waiting to make a left turn onto West 117. In front of him, he noticed an automobile he later described as a dark 1939 Oldsmobile coupe with a man and a young girl inside. The vehicle swung south on West 117 and then turned left onto Linnet Avenue, but immediately exited the street and again headed south. Hess caught a glimpse of an "RE" on the car's license plate. He saw the automobile again, though just when is not clear, parked in a field off Memphis Road; the man, he told police, was beating the young girl. (The Potts files in the homicide unit contain a letter from the Cleveland Automobile Club listing the name and address of every city resident whose license plate either began or ended with "RE," as well as police reports indicating that every person on that list was being checked.)

Beverly's worried parents paced back and forth on the front porch of their home, along with Anita and Betty Morbito, anxiously waiting for the police car to arrive. Suddenly, a taxi pulled up to a house across the street; the Potts family watched as the cab door swung open, hoping desperately that Beverly would emerge from the vehicle. But she didn't; it was only a neighbor returning home. Anita phoned the police a second time. And then a third time. She was on the verge of making a fourth call when a police car finally pulled up to the Potts home, apparently around 12:30 A.M. (The Beverly Potts files contain an official "call-in" slip indicating that someone—most likely Anita placing her third call—had reported Beverly missing at 12:25, Saturday morning.) When the authorities finally arrived at the Potts home, they gave the house two top-to-bottom inspections to make sure Beverly was not hiding there for some unknown reason. "The first thing they did was search the house and yard," Anita remembers, "saying that when little kids come home late, sometimes they hide so their parents don't know they've made it home." Then, operating on the assumption that she may have run away, they checked to see if any of her clothes were missing and inspected her piggy bank to make sure it was intact. At about the same time, word somehow began to spread through the close-knit Linnet Avenue neighborhood—perhaps through the Swing family—that Beverly Potts had not come home. People formed into small groups and joined the fruitless hunt that lasted well into the early morning hours. Fifty years ago, Cleveland neighborhoods behaved like huge extended families; people knew and supported each other. The late-twentieth-century phenomenon of suburban isolation, characterized by families living next door to each other without really knowing or interacting, had yet to develop. Methodically, neighborhood residents wandered the streets and the backyards, carefully checking behind garages and around bushes—all those familiar, "secret" places where their children played and sometimes hid. But there was nothing. The lights in the house at 11304 Linnet Avenue burned on through the night and into the morning, until dawn washed away the darkness and their lonely, silent vigil.

NOTES

The epigraph on page 25 originally appeared as, "She his vanished into nothing," but I have corrected the typo. Ben R. Tidyman was the *Cleveland Plain Dealer*'s chief police reporter.

A Showagon was an old-fashioned form of summer entertainment in neighborhood parks that showcased the talents of local youngsters and, occasionally, adults. Children, mostly teens, would audition for a spot on the roster and be hired for a two-week stint of performances in city playgrounds. The vast majority of the young talent would be driven to and from the designated location by their parents. A city worker would be assigned to transport participants who would otherwise be without a ride. After the two-week tour ended, a new set of acts would begin making the rounds. The productions were all strictly amateur and very low tech.

Patsy Swing's assertion that classmate Robert Bloor remained the only male object of Beverly's ten-year-old affections is contained in a police report of August 29, 1951.

My account of the events on the evening of August 24 is drawn from Cleveland's three major dailies, August 25–September 14, as well as from the existing police reports covering the same period, and from my conversations with Anita Potts, Fred Krause, and Detective Robert Wolf. More specifically, Doris O'Donnell Beaufait's article detailing Patsy Swing's version of what happened that night appeared in the *News* on August 28. The account of Fred Krause's sighting of Beverly after the show first appeared in the September 3 *News;* John G. Blair's sixth anniversary *Plain Dealer* article, published on August 19, 1957, supplies further details concerning Fred Krause's actions after he left Halloran Park.

There are some time discrepancies among the three Cleveland papers involving the exact sequence of events at Halloran on the night of August 24, and the reports in the Beverly Potts files tend to compound the problems created. Initially, I relied on the timeline printed in the *Cleveland News* on both Tuesday, August 28, and Wednesday,

August 29 (reprinted on Friday, August 31, and several times more during the first half of September), partly out of respect for the obvious seriousness of the paper's coverage and also because, to me, it seems the more probable. The paper also offered its definitive sequence of events four days after Beverly's disappearance, thus allowing time to catch and correct the errors that invariably crept into the initial reports as a result of the rush to get an edition on the street. I have, however, freely amended the *News's* chronology with information and time references gathered from the existing police reports. I had to be flexible, not to say vague, when providing specific times for incidents in the text because that was the only way I could account for all the details enumerated in official documents, as well as those covered by the press. Generally, I assumed a range of fifteen minutes in which a reported incident or sighting could have occurred.

There are also some major disagreements as to who did what and when once it became clear Beverly was missing. Though there is general agreement that Anita Potts phoned the Swing home, one version of the story maintained that Elizabeth Potts had actually placed the call—a supposition that Anita firmly rejects. There are also disagreements as to when Anita phoned the Swings—at 9:30, 10:00, sometime in between, or even later—and, as I state in the text, as to whether she went to check Halloran Park by herself or in the company of her father. There are also two different "official" stories as to what Robert Potts did after he and Anita returned home. An early account in the *News* states he walked the neighborhood; later versions insist he drove the family car. As I point out in the text, Anita dismisses both versions. (She also expresses doubts about the claim, reported in all three Cleveland papers, that neighbors joined the hunt for Beverly in the early morning hours of Saturday, August 25. If, however, she was in the house with her mother, she may have remained unaware that others were systematically roaming the neighborhood looking for her sister.) As before, I have regarded the events as set out and described by the *News* beginning on August 28 as the most probable, though I have made revisions in the paper's account with details given to me directly by Anita Potts and with pieces of information drawn from the raw footage of her November 2003 interview with Mark Wade Stone of Storytellers Media Group.

Tangled Threads

It's all so unreal.
Elizabeth Potts to the Cleveland Press, *August 25*

Cleveland Press editor Louis B. Seltzer wrestled with a major dilemma; his go-for-the-jugular journalistic instincts were at war with his conscience. There were reports coming in to the *Press* offices that a little girl had disappeared from Halloran Park the night before, during or following a Showagon performance, and that an intense all-night search mounted by her family, neighbors, and the Cleveland police had failed to turn up a thing. She simply had vanished. On the one hand, it was the sort of heart-wrenching story that the paper could run with in its ongoing campaign to build circulation numbers; on the other hand, the *Press* had cosponsored the event, and lingering embarrassment at least suggested that the paper might be smart to play down the story. It was a battle that the yellow journalist in Seltzer won easily.

Seltzer's rags-to-riches climb up the journalism ladder of success was the stuff of Hollywood and American legend. He had entered the newspaper business in 1909 at the age of twelve. He put in time as a police beat reporter at the *Press* and became editor of the daily in 1928. On the one hand, he was a kingmaker, wielding as much clout in the city as any political boss; on the other hand, he saw himself as a champion of the little guy—a crusader for the rights of the common man. But first and foremost, he knew how to sell papers. By 1951 he had become a Cleveland institution, one of the most powerful men in the city. Seltzer's instincts for shaping and selling, even creating, the news rivaled those of arch competitor William Randolph Hearst. The *Press* would keep the Beverly Potts story on its front pages for weeks.

The *Press* launched its barrage of intensive coverage in the afternoon edition of Saturday, August 25: "Fear West Side Girl Abducted: Police Think Child Is Held Prisoner," screamed the headlines. The *News* chimed in on a less hysterical note with its own headline account: "Fear Missing West Side Girl Kidnapped." Cleveland's morning paper, the *Plain Dealer*, had already gone to press when the story of the missing ten-year-old broke; so the city's respectable, staid daily had to wait until Sunday—a day when neither the *Press* nor the *News* published—to add its more restrained voice to the somber chord: "Seek Two Cars as Girl Hunt Widens."

One of the two automobiles referred to was, of course, the black coupe—now described as a "hot rod"—that several park visitors remembered seeing near Beverly, or someone who looked like her, sometime between 9:00 and 9:30. The other car was a relatively new green model, driven by a man of about fifty. On Thursday evening, the day before the show, both car and driver had terrified Patricia Nagg—a friend of Beverly's who lived at 11425 Linnet Avenue—and some of her friends at Halloran Park. According to her father, Steve, his frightened twelve-year-old daughter reported that this auto had slowly stalked her and her companions, and though the driver never left the car, he followed the girls with his eyes until they ran to the safety of the shelter house. (Patricia Nagg also reported seeing a young man simulating copulation during the Showagon performance Friday evening. This is apparently an entirely unrelated incident.)

Initially, reports of the two men in the old black coupe seemed the most promising lead. Police initially focused their attention on thirteen-year-old Carol Katrenick of Dale Avenue because her memories of the mystery auto seemed the most detailed. She had earlier noticed the car slowly driving up and down her street; she saw the vehicle a couple of times during the evening of August 24 and had even passed by it as she walked home to get a sweater. She insisted to the police that she had seen it in the park area around 9:25, but by 9:35, though she did not see it leave, it had vanished. (Authorities later showed Carol pictures of various car models to see if they could pin down the make and year. That impressive stack of photos is still part of the Beverly Potts files.) A few days after Beverly's disappearance, a mysterious black car cruised slowly around the neighborhood, frightening both Donna Kensick and her best friend, Edie Murton, as they wandered down the street, the girls reported. They ran home quickly, but their parents, interestingly enough, played down the potential significance of the encounter.

"Beverly must have been seized and dragged away," her mother insisted to the *Press* through her tears on August 25. "She's being held by someone. Beverly is too shy to go along willingly. She would have resisted, she would have squirmed and fought terribly. She was so shy nothing could have enticed her to go along with anyone. And Beverly had been earnestly warned many times about talking with strange persons. Someone grabbed her as she walked home from the playground." Elizabeth Potts's cousin Betty Morbito expressed identical sentiments to the *News* on the same day: "I'm sure she would not stay away from home, unless someone was holding her. She was looking forward to the picnic [the reported family outing to Euclid Beach Park] with such pleasure and planned to be in bed early." But potential problems with such a scenario arose immediately. It wasn't just an issue of the time element (conflicting versions of the coupe sighting placed it anywhere from 8:30 to, perhaps, as late as 10:00), nor was it a question of whether Beverly would even talk to the occupants of the mystery auto (some reports insisted she did), let alone get into the car willingly, unless she knew at least one of them; the primary difficulty for the authorities was simply one of opportunity. No one saw the girl who witnesses identified as Beverly get into the old car, and how could anything untoward, such as Elizabeth Potts and Betty Morbito envisioned, have occurred in the midst of such a huge milling crowd? Anita Potts put her finger on the problem and offered a plausible solution to the *News* on August 25. "I'm afraid someone picked her up while she was on her way home from the park. There were too many people in the park for anything out of the way to have happened there." If the two men in the black coupe were, indeed, somehow involved in Beverly's disappearance, then the mysterious vehicle must have followed her from Halloran, or at least met up with her later as she walked east on the dark street that led to her home—thus raising the chilling possibility that she had been grabbed literally within sight of the family house.

The size of the crowd at Halloran Park that Friday evening remains an extremely significant issue. Most accounts place attendance at between one thousand and fifteen hundred. How could anything have happened in the midst of such a large gathering? How or when could Beverly have become isolated enough for an alleged abduction to take place? What is not clear, however, is whether or not all those visitors were in Halloran at the same time. Did the entire crowd stay for the whole show and then break up and leave in a mass, or did people come and go in a constant stream through the evening? Though it may be logical to assume that having made the decision to go to Halloran Park rather than watch or listen to the baseball game at home, most people would have stayed for the entire show, but young children growing weary or bored may have prompted many families to leave early. How many people were actually left in the park when the Showagon performance ended between 9:30 and 9:45? Most of the attendees? Only a few hold-outs? But again a question arises: even if the crowd had largely dispersed, why didn't someone see something? Beverly Potts and Patsy Swing were not the only Linnet Avenue residents to attend the show at Halloran Park that night—though Patsy did insist that they saw no one they recognized. Is it conceivable that no one else—not even a lone straggler—was wandering east on the street at the same time Beverly was heading home, assuming she made it that far? Unless, of course, she had lingered at the park, for whatever reason, long after the show had ended and was, therefore, entirely alone as she walked home. "It's terribly dark at night along here," Anita reiterated to the *Press* on August 27. "Whatever happened, happened right on this street while Beverly was on her way home."

When newsboy Fred Krause came forward on September 3, a week following Beverly's disappearance, and identified the girl he saw who walked like a duck heading toward the West 117–Linnet Avenue intersection as possibly being Beverly Potts, his account became crucial because it placed her in a particular place, at a particular time, in a very particular set of circumstances. She was walking in a northeasterly direction on the grass, heading diagonally across the park toward the West 117–Linnet Avenue intersection shortly after the show ended. In other words, she was surrounded by a large number of people all leaving the park at more or less the same time. For police, therefore, the problem became one of how anything as potentially violent as an abduction could have occurred given that set of circumstances. If Beverly had been kidnapped against her will, then that act had had to occur at a time when, and a place where, she would have been relatively alone. And given the reported circumstances, there was virtually no window of opportunity. (It's also highly unlikely that anything out of the ordinary could have happened so close to a street as heavily traveled as West 117.) A modern suburban resident will have difficulty understanding just how small and compact an area the Linnet Avenue neighborhood is and how short the distances are between one point and the next. It is an old residential city neighborhood (the Potts home was built in 1927), and by the standards of today's suburbs, the street is extremely narrow. Many of the houses are little bigger than cottages; even the homes in the inner ring of older Cleveland suburbs are larger and farther apart. A present-day suburbanite would also characterize the front lawns of Linnet Avenue as postage stamps. Someone standing in front of his or her house was literally only a few feet away from the sidewalk. Even a slow amble from the Potts residence at 11304 to Halloran Park on the other side of West 117 Street would take little more than five minutes. One need only stand on Linnet Avenue today and carefully survey the surroundings to understand how utterly mystifying Beverly's disappearance was and is— the houses are so close to each other and so close to the street, and the distance from the Potts residence to the park so short. There are and were no empty lots, no vacant spaces or gaps. The entire neighborhood seems small, tight, even claustrophobic. No matter how total the darkness along Linnet Avenue, how could anything even remotely out of the ordinary have happened without someone seeing something—someone on the street, in a front yard, on a porch—even in a front window?

Assuming the girl Fred Krause saw that night was, indeed, Beverly, heading diagonally across Halloran in a northeasterly direction toward her Linnet Avenue home, once at the West 117–Linnet Avenue intersection she would most likely have crossed the major thoroughfare to the south side of Linnet. The Potts home, however, stood on the north side of the street. Assuming she had made it that far, exactly where might she have been when she crossed from the south side of Linnet to the north side? Most of the time, there was very little traffic on Linnet Avenue, and it seems logical to assume she may have simply drifted across the street on the diagonal toward her house. But there was, and still is, a neighborhood tavern on the southeast corner of West 117 and Linnet; in those days, it was known as Walter's Bar and, though hardly the 1950s equivalent of a biker bar, some children in the neighborhood felt uneasy around it and generally gave it a wide berth. Beverly's sense of caution would probably have prompted her to cross to the north side almost immediately. (Mr. Fred Kohl's deli and candy store stood on the northeast corner of the intersection.) If she did remain on the south side of the street, the possibility that she may have been waylaid by someone leaving the bar begins to loom large. If, however, she was walking on the north side of Linnet, then any automobile that may have intercepted her would most likely have been traveling in a westerly direction. But Fred Krause's mother, Dorothy, was standing in front of the family residence on the north side of Linnet at 11500 from 8:30 until around 10:30, waiting for her son and husband to return. (According to reports, Fred joined her after he arrived home sometime between 9:45 and 10:00.) Granted, she surely did not stand before the house like a statue for two solid hours, arms folded across her chest and eyes locked on the street. She may have puttered in the yard, wandered around to the back of the house, or even gone inside for a short time. But she was outside during an extremely crucial period of time, and she insisted that she saw no one on the street. Yet Patsy Swing walked by the Krause home on her way home at approximately 8:45; and between then and 10:30, Martin Pilot and his wife (close to 9:00), Mary Hunt and her three grandsons (between 9:30 and 10:15), Gloria Vrana and Patricia Kovar (around 10:00), as well as Robert Potts and his daughter Anita (also around 10:00 or so) passed by the Krause residence. Dorothy Krause apparently did not see any of them. In the 1950s police officers rarely editorialized in their reports, yet one document specifically points to the inherent contradictions in the accounts provided by Dorothy Krause and Mary Hunt. (In fairness, I must also point out that none of the people passing the Krause home specifically remembered seeing Dorothy in front of the house.) Gloria Vrana and Patricia Kovar sat on the Vrana front porch at 11512 Linnet from sometime around 10:00 to 10:30, and apparently neither one of them saw anyone walking on the sidewalks in either direction.

Given the reported circumstances, it is virtually inconceivable that anything strange or violent could have happened, without anyone's noticing, before Beverly crossed West 117. Given the proximity of the Krause residence to the intersection, it is almost impossible to understand why neither Dorothy nor her son noticed Beverly pass by—again, assuming the girl he saw at Halloran was, indeed, Beverly—if she was following so closely behind Fred as he bicycled home. There are, of course, a number of variables to which we will never know the answers. How fast was Fred Krause traveling? Was Beverly walking quickly or simply ambling along when he said he pedaled up behind her? Was the light in Fred's favor when he arrived at the intersection? Even if not, would a teenager on a bicycle wait for the traffic light to change—thus, perhaps, allowing for the bulk of the crowd to catch up with him—or would he have bolted across the street at the first opportunity, light or no light? Was the same traffic light in Beverly's favor? If not, chances are she would have waited for it to change. How close behind Fred Krause was she? Did Dorothy follow her son up the driveway to the back yard when he arrived home, wait for him to park his bike, and then walk with him back to the front of the house? Such a scenario might allow enough time for Beverly to pass by unseen. But that would also mean that whatever happened had to occur very quickly between the Krause home at 11500 and the Potts residence at 11304. A very small window of opportunity, indeed.

Or is it conceivable that Fred Krause may have been in error as to whom he saw or when he saw her? Is it possible that Beverly had left Halloran earlier than reported—that the lateness and darkness of the hour, perhaps even the chill in the air, prompted her to leave before the show ended, conceivably shortly after Patsy Swing went home? Fifty years ago, local newspapers were not inclined to dilute the power of a good story with qualifiers, especially when that story was tied to such a sensational case; so Fred Krause's identification of Beverly walking toward the West 117–Linnet Avenue intersection at the close of the show was played as an absolute certainty. At the time, no one in the press saw any reason to question his assertion. After all, he saw her in the neighborhood frequently. He also delivered the *Press* to the Potts house, and Beverly occasionally paid him. Today, Fred Krause remembers how shy she was, how she never looked him in the face but invariably dropped her head and averted her glance. The police accepted his identification. "They asked me why I thought it was Beverly," he recalls, "and I said, 'because she walked like a duck.' And that ended it." Today, however, more than fifty years later, the former newspaper boy and neighbor is less sure. "I thought I saw her," he reflects. "I remember telling my mother I might have seen her." Krause remains positive, however, that he did, indeed, see Beverly earlier in the evening during the show and that he rode up behind the girl he later identified as possibly being Beverly as the crowd left Halloran Park. If, however, he was mistaken about whom he saw, then it is certainly possible that Beverly had already headed for home, thus conceivably placing her in a relatively isolated spot just long enough for something potentially violent to happen.

Chief of detectives James E. McArthur was a battle-hardened, soft-spoken, twenty-year veteran of the Cleveland Police Department. He joined the force on November 5, 1931, and rose steadily through the ranks, being appointed deputy inspector in 1948 and chief of detectives in 1949. He

Inspector James E. McArthur, chief of detectives. He began working the case on Saturday, August 25, 1951, the morning the Potts family reported Beverly missing. He would eventually lead the largest manhunt in Cleveland history. He could be gruff and short tempered, but his devotion to the case and the emotional well-being of the Potts family was total. In the months following Beverly's disappearance, he would work himself to exhaustion. *Plain Dealer* Collection, Cleveland Public Library.

was a thin, gaunt-faced man who carried himself with the aristocratic bearing of a Prussian military officer sporting a "von" before his last name; even in plain clothes, he conducted himself as if he still wore a uniform. He was tough, and he was proud of his badge. "He loved the job," remembers reporter Doris O'Donnell Beaufait. "A wonderful man," reflects Anita Potts warmly. "Kind and thoughtful!" Delmar O'Hare, a thirty-year veteran of the force—1946 to 1976—recalls a "straight-laced" man who "never seemed very happy." In an August 29 *News* portrait of McArthur, reporter Sanford Sobul described a "crisp" personality infused with a streak of nervousness that quickly turned into irritability when he faced a "complete riddle." "To more than any other type of crime, 'Jim' McArthur reacts with a vengeance in cases involving children," Sobul wrote. "Inspector McArthur hates crimes involving children because they sicken him as no other crimes do." During his twenty-year career, McArthur had routinely given 100 percent and more to every case on which he had worked. There is no surviving record as to when or how he came to head up the investigation into the Beverly Potts disappearance, but by 7:00 A.M. Saturday, the morning after she vanished, he was on the job. Every police officer faces the possibility that during his career that one special case may come along—one that will frustrate and consume him, one that will absorb every moment of his professional life and darken his personal life as well. For detective Peter Merylo in the 1930s, it had been the Kingsbury Run murders; for chief of detectives James E. McArthur, it would be the disappearance of Beverly Potts.

Every deep mystery inevitably cloaks a series of smaller ones—conundrums, questions, details, and pieces of the puzzle that contribute to the fabric of the legend without being examined too closely. One such unanswered riddle in the Beverly Potts case remains James McArthur's participation at such an early stage. By Saturday morning, Beverly had been missing for only about ten hours; it was certainly not clear whether she had, indeed, been abducted or simply run away. Why would someone of such high rank become involved in what seemed at this point a garden variety missing-child case when there was no evidence that a crime had even been committed? *News* reporter Sanford Sobul's contention that crimes against children simply pushed McArthur's buttons is not enough to explain his presence on the scene by Saturday morning. Though at the time no one in the media seems to have regarded his early involvement as needing any comment (indeed, no one questioned it publicly), sources within the Cleveland Police Department have told me that McArthur's active participation at this point would be regarded as "highly unusual" by present-day standards. The simplest explanation for McArthur's presence is that Louis B. Seltzer gave one of the levers of power to which he enjoyed such easy access a mighty yank. If he felt any guilt by association for his paper's cosponsorship of the Showagon performance, he could salve that itch by pressuring Chief of Police George J. Matowitz to assign his top man to the case. Opinions may differ as to whether Matowitz was an inspired leader or simply a competent figurehead, but he was the longest-serving chief in departmental history, having been appointed in 1931. He was, therefore, an institution in his own right. But he was nearing the end of his lengthy tenure—he died in November 1951—and may have been especially vulnerable to the pressure of a powerful local press lord used to getting his own way. There may be legitimate questions as to whether Seltzer actually had that kind of clout in the police department, but no one doubts that if he did have it, he used it.

McArthur immediately dismissed the notion that Beverly might have run away. "From all that we can learn, she was not that type," McArthur told the *Plain Dealer* on August 26, a position he vehemently reasserted to the *Press* two days later. "I cannot accept any theory that Beverly ran away. She lived in a happy home and had no desire or reason to go off." "I think Beverly Potts was taken away in an automobile by a person or persons she knew well enough to talk to," he declared to the *Press* on August 29. "Every bit of evidence in this case, every report and every conversation leads to the conclusion that Beverly absolutely would not have gone anywhere with a stranger. There may have been another or others in the car. But the one who first spoke to Beverly was not a stranger. Had he been, she would have run up the street." If Beverly had gotten into a car willingly, she must have been lured by someone she knew and trusted—someone who, perhaps, had promised her a babysitting job or asked her to run some sort of errand. McArthur insisted that his scenario remained the only explanation that made any sense given the circumstances surrounding her disappearance. He pointed out, just as Anita Potts had, that absolutely nothing violent or even remotely out of the ordinary could have taken place at the park with so many people wandering the area. No one had heard an outcry. "And remember too, there were folks from Beverly's block on Linnet Ave. who were going and coming from that playground before, during and after the show." On two points, however, McArthur's carefully reasoned analysis falters: though witnesses placed her at the side of the car talking to the men or boys inside, no one saw Beverly get into it. Second, family members described Beverly as an extremely shy child, especially around men and boys, even those she knew. According to Elizabeth Potts's niece, Eileen Treuer Lathan, Beverly could actually appear "unfriendly" to people she did not know. Beverly had known Patsy Swing's father for most of her life, yet she always seemed slightly timid around him and rarely spoke to him. If she had been snatched by strangers, could she have been too surprised or too frightened to cry out for help? Whether the dark forebodings that would haunt McArthur had gained a hold from the moment he took command of the investigation on August 25 is unclear, but very early on he came to a painful conclusion, one that he kept to himself for at least a couple of days before confiding to the *Press* on August 27: "I fear the little girl may be dead."

By early Saturday morning, mounted policemen, other uniformed officers, detectives, every available police cruiser, and members of two different Boy Scout troops fanned out from Halloran Park, scouring the neighborhoods, fields, and parks as far away as Big Creek, Edgewater

The beginning of a search that still continues more than a half century later.
Cleveland mounted police in the Metro Parks. *Cleveland Press* Archives, Cleveland
State University.

Park, and the Rocky River Reservation (recreational areas west of the
city); but they turned up nothing save a seventy-year-old vagrant—later
determined to be uninvolved—asleep in a field. City firemen, the Civil
Air Patrol, and employees from the city park and service division would
also join the organized hunt (though exactly when these groups became involved is not entirely clear), swelling the army of searchers to
twelve hundred, according to a *News* estimate on August 29. Authorities
asked New York Central railroad police to search all the boxcars on the
Linndale sidings close to the Potts home. Beverly's picture flashed across
local television screens throughout the day.

The police alerted the FBI that a child was missing, but provisions in
the law enacted after the Lindbergh kidnapping kept the bureau from
active participation: what the bureau needed was a ransom note or a
telephone call from the abductors. Ray J. Abbaticchio, special agent in
charge of the Cleveland field division for the FBI, told the *Plain Dealer*
on August 28, "There has been no indication or evidence of an actual

kidnaping [*sic*] which would give the federal government jurisdiction to make an active investigation." (In cases of verified kidnapping, if the abducted child is not returned unharmed within seven days, the FBI assumes the victim has been transported across state lines. If it turns out that no federal offence actually has been committed, then the bureau will turn over whatever information it has gathered to local authorities.) Though the FBI could not take an active role in the local investigation, within a week of Beverly's disappearance the bureau had promised to print her picture and an account of the supposed abduction in *FBI Crime Reports* (at the time, the nation's largest such publication) and had sent out twenty-two thousand circulars over the entire country containing both her photograph and description.

Then the reports of Beverly Potts sightings all over Cuyahoga County and as far away as Kansas City and Baltimore began flooding into the Central Police Station. A truck driver believed he had seen her in a car with two men heading toward Elyria on Route 20 at 10:00 A.M. Saturday morning, approximately thirteen hours after she disappeared; at the same time, W. I. Gates, a New York Central engineer who lived on West 11, was sure he had seen her with a fourteen-year-old boy trying to hitch a ride near Brookpark and Tiedeman Roads, a couple of miles southeast of Halloran Park. In both instances, McArthur doubted that the girl that witnesses had seen was actually Beverly Potts. Three days later on Monday, August 28, Clarence E. Kyle of West 48 saw a girl who resembled Beverly and a fourteen-year-old boy walking west along the Nickel Plate railroad tracks as he crossed over a bridge at West 53. When he shouted at the pair, they bolted and were ultimately hidden by a passing train. They appeared "mussed up," Kyle reported to the *Press* on August 29, "as though they had been sleeping out." Gates's and Kyle's sightings clearly demonstrate the grinding frustrations Cleveland police faced. Even assuming both stories are accurate, were the youngsters Kyle saw along the rails the same pair that Gates observed at Brookpark and Tiedeman? Is it even remotely possible that the young girl in either sighting was Beverly Potts? In Hudson, a small town thirty miles southeast of Cleveland, Elizabeth Potts's cousin Mrs. Irene Carney watched in amazement on Sunday as a car with two men and a girl passed by her Miller Road home, the young passenger waving merrily. Although she did not recognize either of the two men, Beverly had been to her house for a few days a short time before, and Carney thought the young female passenger could be her Cousin Elizabeth's daughter.

Unfortunately, many of the reports police had to deal with seemed vague, sketchy, even improbable. According to the August 29 *Press*, a twelve-year-old boy supposedly shared a secret with his friend John Billingsly: he had given a "jumpy and nervous" Beverly a ride on his bike from Halloran to West 117 and Belaire Road "to keep an appointment" on the night she disappeared. (He placed the curious errand at 8:00 P.M., a full forty-five minutes before Patsy Swing left Beverly to go home.) Frank Emery, an elevator operator at Lakeside Courthouse, reported to the *Press* on the same day that he had given an elevator ride to a "dirty-faced" and "weary" seeming girl dressed like Beverly at about 3:00 P.M. the day before on August 28. The *Plain Dealer* reported on August 29 that a West Side woman insisted that she had received a phone call from a young girl who announced, "This is Beverly Potts. Tell my mother I'm all right and will meet her at East 13 Street and Chester." A couple of boys told police they had seen a car with a man asleep in the front seat and a "small figure" in the back. No doubt police were seriously tempted to practice some sort of triage on all the swirling rumors, separating the promising tips from the seemingly less plausible. (McArthur even implored the parents of girls around Beverly's age not to dress their children in blue jeans, blue jackets, and reddish-pink shirts while the investigation was going on.) The only course open to authorities, however, was to check all such reports as thoroughly as possible—a brutally slow, time-consuming process, when nothing seemed more important than speed.

An intense hush hovered over Linnet Avenue on Saturday. All along the street, people stood quietly on their front porches, watching and waiting. Weary neighbors who had searched unsuccessfully through the night for the missing girl stood around in groups wondering what to do next. Slowly, inevitably, the stark truth of what had happened began to cut deep into the neighborhood psyche, shattering the collective sense of security: one of their own, a little girl whom everyone seemed to know and like, had vanished amid circumstances that defied explanation. As the morning wore on, the vanguard of an invading army of law-enforcement personnel, reporters, and photographers began to infiltrate the quiet street and take up their positions. Police and newspaper men wandered in the midst of the large crowd forming in front of the Potts home. The question on everyone's lips was "why." "Why would anyone want to pick on little Beverly?" asked Mrs. Thomas Fahey. "She was such a cute little trick. It breaks my heart." "Why does this have to happen to these

Worry turns to panic: the women of Linnet Avenue. From left to right: Peggy Fahey, Ann Kilbane, Ann Cossano, Helen Eiben, and Murrielle Cassak. *Cleveland Press* Archives, Cleveland State University.

people?" interjected neighbor Joe Eiben. A group of friends and neighbors gathered on the porch; some went in the house to offer what comfort and support they could. Some brought food; others answered the constantly ringing telephone. Among those who called to offer encouragement was Mrs. Katharine Michel of Lakewood, whose daughter Gail Ann had been abducted a few weeks before by a man described as a "sex deviant" by the *Press,* only to be released eighteen hours later. And there were other random acts of kindness from strangers. An unidentified elderly man elbowed his way through the crowd carrying a message of hope for the Potts family. Fifteen years before, his nine-year-old daughter had been kidnapped, held in the country, and beaten, until her abductor mysteriously released her three days later. A happy ending was always possible.

Inside the house, relatives and friends wandered about trying to seem busy, frequently passing by Beverly's cardboard dollhouse, surrounded by her collection of dolls, which stood off to one side—everything just as she had left it. (Newspaper accounts differ as to whether the dollhouse stood in the living room or the dining room, on a table or on the floor. Though it remains difficult to ascertain which room, press photographs indicate it was on a table next to a wall.) As her parents slipped deeper into debilitating worry and despair, Anita Potts gradually took over the running of the household. Robert Potts chain-smoked during the brief rest periods he allowed himself when he wasn't searching the neighborhood alone or riding with the police. "You think you know how parents feel when you read about such things in the newspapers," he mused to *Plain Dealer* reporter Pat Garling. "But it's impossible." He refused to sleep. Elizabeth Potts had managed only a couple of hours of fitful slumber. Though relatives had called in a doctor to help her rest, she had resisted. "I'm waiting," she explained. "I don't want to sleep." Outside, evening drifted over the usually quiet street. It had been twenty-four

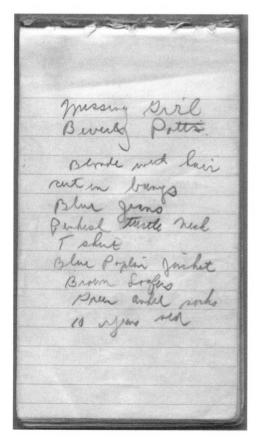

A page from the notebook of officer Raymond Mickol, recording Beverly's description. Though undated, the entry was probably made on the morning of Saturday, August 25 during roll call. Cleveland Police Historical Society Museum.

hours since Beverly vanished, and the darker, less charitable reactions to the Potts family tragedy were slowly taking shape. The friends and neighbors standing in front of the house watched silently as the long lines of cars began to creep by—the curious, inquisitive faces turned to the house where the missing child lived.

NOTES

I have pieced together the events of August 25 from the coverage in Cleveland's three daily papers, August 25–August 31, and from surviving police reports covering the same period. Detective Robert Wolf of the Cleveland Police Department led me through the published timeline of Beverly's disappearance step by step, calling my attention to details that needed to be questioned or looked at more closely. It should, for example, be noted that Fred Krause waited ten days before he publicly shared with anyone his story of bicycling up behind Beverly at the show's close. He, or someone else, also seems to have passed it on initially to the newspapers, not the police. The *News* broke the story on September 3; a police report dated the same day states that authorities did not question Fred directly until after 4:30 that afternoon—by which time the paper would have already been on the streets. Did Cleveland police actually learn of Fred Krause's eyewitness account from the *Cleveland News?* When I interviewed Fred Krause for the first time on July 21, 2003, I asked him why he had waited so long before coming forward. "I don't know," he responded thoughtfully. "Maybe, I was afraid. I was just a kid."

The portrait of James McArthur is drawn from personal interviews with Delmar O'Hare, Doris O'Donnell Beaufait, and Anita Potts. As stated in the text, I also relied heavily on Sanford Sobul's August 29 *News* profile of the chief of detectives.

The accounts of Beverly's extreme shyness around men and boys were given to detective Robert Wolf by the former Patricia Ann Swing in the year 2000.

The fullest accounts of conditions in and around the Potts household on the first day of the search remain Pat Garling's *Plain Dealer* article of August 26 and a similar piece in the August 27 issue of the *Press*.

The Politics of Abduction

Beverly, if you are free please come home—we miss you so very much.
An appeal by Elizabeth Potts broadcast on a WGAR radio news program

Late Sunday night on August 26, Beverly Potts's disappearance became the business of Cleveland city government; both Mayor Thomas A. Burke and safety director Alvin J. Sutton became publicly involved. Late that evening, Burke handed a search plan over to public service director Samuel F. David and public properties director Arthur L. Munson calling for the deployment of around eight hundred city workers to aid police in the hunt for the missing child. Sutton's role would be somewhat more ceremonial; he was to be "regularly informed" on the progress made in the investigation.

Burke's plan, actually James McArthur's brainchild, would pull a large contingent of men from the garbage collection division and send them to the wooded areas south of Halloran Park to participate in the search effort. Others would concentrate on exploring alleys and gullies, though exactly where was not specified in newspaper accounts. Still more of the men under David's supervision, presumably more garbage collectors, would be asked to keep their eyes open for anything significant or suspicious while they made their regular rounds. Sewer workers would be sent into the Big Creek culvert running from West 117 to West 130 Street. Munson's park division men would fan out and search every inch of all the city park areas. Though officially authorities were still operating on the assumption that Beverly had been abducted, for the first time newspapers raised the possibility that she may have met with some sort of unfortunate accident in the rugged terrain surrounding Halloran Park, especially to the south.

Earlier in the day, *Plain Dealer* reporter Leonard Hammer hopped on board one of the two planes from the Civil Air Patrol's Fifth Cleveland Squadron as they rose into the gray skies from Cleveland Hopkins Airport to conduct an aerial search. Initially, pilot and operations officer Lieutenant Denes Ferencz concentrated on the areas close to the Potts home on Linnet Avenue. Hammer gulped and broke into a mild sweat when Ferencz took the plane down low enough so they could clearly see people on the ground looking up and waving merrily. He noticed a lone police car parked on Briggs Avenue; officers were canvassing the entire neighborhood door to door, inquiring whether anyone had seen a little girl dressed as Beverly had been dressed the night she disappeared. Cruising at an altitude of five hundred feet at a comfortable fifty miles an hour, the plane followed the path of Big Creek south of Halloran Park and checked close to one hundred open coal cars at the Linndale Station railroad yards. Suddenly, the enormity of the task facing searchers on the ground overwhelmed Hammer; his heart sank as he looked down on a seemingly endless procession of wild undergrowth, steep cliffs, woods, trash dumps, and other largely remote areas close to the Potts home that remained "impossible to search with less than a regiment." The sheer number of places where a body could be hidden staggered both Ferencz and Hammer. "To this reporter," he wrote in the *Plain Dealer* the next day, "it was amazing how much desolate acreage lay within walking distance of the youngster's home in the heart of this busy metropolis." The entire aerial exploration had been McArthur's idea, and he asked Lieutenant Charles B. Kemp—commander of air rescue for the Fourth Cleveland Civil Air Patrol Group—to keep both planes ready to resume the search over a wider area on Monday. At the end of his flight, Hammer mused that he and pilot Ferencz "saw no signs of life" in the rugged desolation they had explored, "—or happily, of death."

The *Press* apparently sought to atone for having cosponsored the Showagon performance at which Beverly had disappeared by covering the story in detail and vigorously crusading on its front pages for total public cooperation with the police; it had taken the lead and set the tone. And in the 1950s, the competition among the city's three major dailies was so fierce that the *News* and the *Plain Dealer* were virtually obliged to follow suit, even though their editors and publishers may have shuddered at the often super-charged level of their competitor's rhetoric. However, strong the sense of competition from the generals in the boardrooms and at the city desks, the brotherhood among the soldier-journalists in the trenches remained strong. Reporters on the police beat, as well as other writers and photographers from all three Cleveland dailies—Doris O'Donnell Beaufait and Bill Petersen from the *News*, Sam Giamo, Bus Bergen, and Ben Marino from the *Press*—joined the crowds outside the Potts home. They found a neighborhood both deeply traumatized and strangely schizophrenic. Terrified residents kept their children inside and only spoke to reporters reluctantly, if at all. On one hand, Beverly Potts was a well-known neighborhood favorite, and the tight-knit Linnet Avenue community had come together on the night she disappeared to search for the missing girl; on the other hand, people assumed that if she had, indeed, been snatched by a "pervert," there was a strong possibility that person lived nearby, perhaps even on Linnet Avenue. (If Beverly had been lured into the house of someone she at least recognized, that would explain why no one had heard any outcry.) Hence residents grew deeply suspicious of any neighbors whom they did not know well. Over time, it would become clear that at least some of that suspicion was directed at the Potts household, itself—most of it apparently stemming from the fact that Robert Potts kept rather odd hours because of his erratic work schedule, and he was not particularly well known to his neighbors. (Though they never found a reason to implicate him in his daughter's disappearance, police would subject Robert Potts, as well as other members of the household, to intense, almost invasive, scrutiny.)

By Sunday morning, James McArthur had been up for more than twenty-four hours, and reports indicated he was scheduled to take the day off. But at dawn, he was back at Halloran Park—grim-faced, determined, tired, and more gaunt than ever—directing his men in another sweep of the entire area—empty boxcars, ravines, any place where a frightened or injured child—or a dead body—might be trapped or could be hidden. They checked everywhere. The Potts family had supplied authorities with a list of friends and relatives, and inquiries went out as far West Virginia and even Arizona. Police sent letters of inquiry to other police departments all over the country. (The files of the Potts case contain letters from jurisdictions across the country acknowledging the receipt of those letters from Cleveland authorities.) Police identified and interviewed all the performers and technicians involved with the Showagon at Halloran on Friday night. Robert Potts assured authorities that no one in his family had had trouble with any of their neighbors, nor was there anyone in his union who might hold a grudge against him because of some prior disciplinary action. Beverly had never threatened to run away, he insisted. He maintained that he had never hit her; the only trouble he or his wife had ever had with her involved her staying outside after her curfew. Later in the day, McArthur ordered his men to round up every known sex offender, numbering about sixty-five people, on Cleveland's West Side and bring them in for questioning.

The fruitless odyssey of Detective Sergeant Ray Moran and his partner Detective Patrick Lenahan was sadly typical. With photo in hand, they went to the home of a man known for his "sexually irregular" tastes, even though no shred of evidence tied him to the missing girl. At the door, the man's irate father complained that other officers had been there earlier in the day checking and then shouted that his son was in prison for yet another sex offence.

At the Potts home, sheer exhaustion took its inevitable toll, for a time overwhelming even the anxiety and despair that had tortured the family relentlessly since Friday evening. Robert and daughter Anita finally

The grieving mother. A *Press* photographer caught this unbearably poignant picture of Elizabeth Potts in the days following Beverly's disappearance. Friends, family, and well-wishers who gathered in the Potts home reported that she seemed to be crying softly virtually all the time. *Cleveland Press* Archives, Cleveland State University.

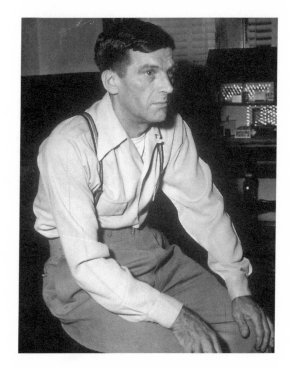

Beverly's father, Robert Potts. He did not show his emotions openly. Reporters who covered the story judged him gruff, distant, and uncommunicative. Beverly's cardboard doll house sits on a table in the background. *Cleveland Press* Archives, Cleveland State University.

fell into five to six hours of fitful slumber, and Elizabeth apparently gave into the entreaties of friends and relatives that she let a doctor give her something to help her sleep. She refused to go to bed, but with the aid of a sedative, she rested Saturday night on a downstairs daybed. In the evening, hopes suddenly flickered to life. Police whisked Anita to West Park Cemetery, where someone had reported seeing a wandering little girl answering Beverly's description, only to find a neighborhood youngster on her way home. Sometime Sunday afternoon or early in the evening—conceivably coming on the heels of dashed hopes after the West Park Cemetery sighting—technicians from radio station WGAR came to 11304 Linnet Avenue to record Elizabeth's desperate appeal for her daughter's return, to be broadcast on the 11:00 P.M. news. "Beverly, if you are free please come home—we miss you so very much," she pleaded. Her voice quavered and broke on the final words, but no one suggested that the frantic mother should rerecord her desperate plea.

Again, the *Press* took up the banner and led the journalistic charge with a bombastic, page-one trumpet blast. "Let's All Join Hunt for Missing Child," ran the headline for an unsigned editorial in the Monday, August 27, edition. "The hearts of thousands of Clevelanders today feel a deep sense of anxiety for the safety of little Beverly Potts." The editorial went on:

This child, who played so happily throughout the day Friday and then vanished, left behind her a fearful mystery which brought to the minds of each and all a wish—and to the lips a prayer—that this nightmare shall pass and Beverly shall be restored to her parents.

We must not yield in frustration to this deep sense of sympathy which a whole city feels for the parents. Instead, we should give it expression in a persistent search that will not end until the mystery is solved.

Each parent knows that it might have been his own child.

Let us unite and find Beverly. Let every person in Greater Cleveland, as he goes about his daily work, keep a sharp lookout for any bit of evidence, however small, that might lead to her discovery. The tiniest clew [sic] may lead to a solution of the mystery.

And God grant that our urgent errand will be rewarded.

The first tangible rewards proffered, however, were strictly monetary. Robert Potts served on the executive board of the Stagehands Union AFL, Local 27, and as an expression of sympathy and support for their colleague and his family, the union offered a $1,500 reward for information leading to the arrest and conviction of Beverly's kidnapper. In a demonstration of continuing civic concern over the plight of the Potts family, Councilmen James Donnelly and Joseph F. Flannery promised they would press city council to adopt a resolution asking the county commissioners to establish a similar monetary incentive. Within days, the sum pledged by the Stagehands Union would grow to $4,050 through additional contributions from the Cleveland Federation of Labor, the Teamsters District Council, the Painters District Council, the Building Trades Council, Electrical Workers' Local 38, Building Service Employees' Local 47, Ticket Sellers and Treasurers' Local 752, Furniture Finishers' Local 725, and the Cuyahoga Tavern Keepers and Liquor Dealers Association. By the end of the month, Cleveland Federation of Labor secretary William Finnegan was campaigning for additional donations to bring the total to $10,000. (By November, the fund stood at approximately $8,000.) Common Pleas Judge James C. Connell was appointed arbiter to oversee the distribution of the money, especially in cases of conflicting claims.

. . .

By Monday, McArthur had still gone virtually without sleep. Regulations would have permitted him to take both Sunday and Monday off, but in a fierce, wholly characteristic display of gritty dedication that Gen. George Patton would have admired, he scuttled family plans to devote his full energies to the investigation. When he wasn't somewhere in the field leading his troops, he directed operations in his office from 5:00 A.M. to 11:00 P.M., hurriedly gobbling meals at his desk, periodically updating Burke on the status of the search, and personally trying to screen the estimated two hundred calls and tips (a volume that would soon swell to between four hundred and five hundred calls per shift— more than fifteen hundred a day) that came in to the detective bureau. (The Potts files contain a daunting list describing the nature of the telephone tips that poured in over a couple of days, including the times they were received.) He contemptuously dismissed most as the work of "cranks and dreamers." A mental telepathist saw Beverly lying in heavy brush; a "dream interpreter" saw her floating in a pool near a street the name of which began with the letter *L;* another tip placed the missing girl in McKeesport, Pennsylvania. Angry women called and fingered former boyfriends for a host of reasons, and perhaps most ominously, some callers insisted the child was hidden in the Potts home—perhaps alive, possibly dead. "They all must be checked out," McArthur lamented to the *Plain Dealer* on August 28. "I know how those parents must feel," he further confided to the *Plain Dealer.* "If I worked all week without stopping I wouldn't suffer as much as the Potts family has in the last five minutes."

Weary and deeply frustrated, McArthur broadcast a public appeal over the radio—similar to, though far less pompous and fervent than, the *Press's* front-page editorial. Parts of his entreaty, however, sound a little journalistically formal for such a blunt-spoken policeman, and it's certainly possible his radio address may have been, at least in part, ghostwritten. "I don't care how insignificant the findings may be considered," he assured listeners. "Maybe 999 tips will prove false leads. It's the next one that's going to lead us to Beverly Potts. Even the most trifling tip might be the one we are looking for and we are willing to listen to anybody and everybody." He further urged listeners to search their own property, especially any empty lots or vacant buildings.

By Monday morning, the investigation had already settled into a numbing routine of searching and interviewing—sometimes interrogating. Interestingly, McArthur told the *Plain Dealer* on Tuesday, August 28, that the police were "feeling their way," because there was simply no precedent for them to go by. Official actions reported by the press, however, make it clear that authorities were adopting a two-pronged course of action: either Beverly lay dead or severely injured in some remote spot, or she was being held in an undisclosed location by her abductors. Though the two positions are not necessarily mutually exclusive, the first assumption obviously guided the bulk of the investigation. The papers never indicated that police may have been waiting for a ransom demand.

For the second day in a row searchers took to the air again on Monday, August 27—this time joined by Aileen Pickering and Irma Story, two female pilots on a national tour to promote the role of women in air defense. For the second day, Hammer went up with the Civil Air Patrol (CAP), this time with pilot CAP Staff Sergeant John A. Schoenbeck. In a well-coordinated air-to-ground search, the tiny red and black plane flew over the remote areas close to Halloran Park and radioed reports of anything suspicious to squad cars on the ground. "We sent police on several fruitless searches," he lamented the next day. A pair of blue jeans, such as Beverly had been wearing, spotted at the base of a fifty-foot cliff on the Erie shore, turned out to have been forgotten by a swimmer. On August 28 the *Plain Dealer* ran two separate accounts of Monday's search, literally side by side—one by Hammer, the other unsigned. The discrepancies between the pair of reports provide a clear example of the seeming confusion that often dogged newspaper coverage and that today create such frustration for anyone trying to piece together exactly what was happening. Both stories agree that someone from the air spotted a green sedan parked on a remote path near the New York Central Railroad Bridge in Brooklyn Heights—Hammer says it was a Nash—matching the description of the mysterious vehicle that had terrorized some of Beverly's friends in Halloran Park the day before she disappeared. Hammer reports that he and Schoenbeck found the car; the unsigned piece assigns the discovery instead to Lieutenant Kemp. Hammer reports that the driver had removed a box from the car and was heading into the woods; the anonymous article says the mysterious man with the box slid down a slope and appeared to scatter something white on the Cuyahoga Valley floor. According to the unsigned piece, Kemp landed his plane and sent another one (the plane containing Hammer and Schoenbeck?) to monitor the scene. Both stories agree that Kemp and another man (Hammer says it was Detective Theodore P. Whittaker) sped to the location spotted from the air. Both articles agree that mystery car and driver were gone by the time the police car (Hammer) or the second plane (unsigned piece) arrived. Though the specifics differ, both also agree that searchers found some clothing and camping equipment that later turned out to belong to some local youngsters planning an outing. (Which story is the more accurate? On one hand, Leonard Hammer's piece is a firsthand account, but on the other hand, the unsigned article quotes Kemp frequently.) McArthur arranged for two National Guard planes to join the hunt if necessary, and five additional patrol planes from Akron, Canton, and Massillon were put on alert for possible service the next day.

On the ground, as in the air, the army of searchers swelled in size, and the hunt rippled out from Halloran Park and Linnet Avenue in ever-expanding circles. Two boys turned over to police a chunk of bloody-looking concrete, along with some similarly stained pebbles, that they had found in a field of rubble at Thrush Avenue. The two mysterious automobiles, one green, the other black, that authorities had been look-ing for since Saturday morning remained elusive. A new contingent of about thirty-five rookie police officers canvassed the streets close to Lin-net Avenue, apparently going door to door interviewing residents again for any possible clue. In addition to Parks employees, garbage collec-tors, and Boy Scouts, West Park postmen were instructed to ask ques-tions of the residents on their rounds. At least a dozen detectives de-voted all their efforts to tracking down known West Side sex offenders for questioning and following up on all the recent reports from women claiming to have been accosted in any way. But McArthur was still not satisfied. "We cannot any longer concentrate on the area around the Potts home, or even on the West Side," McArthur told the army of search-ers according to the *Press* on August 27. "Too much time has elapsed. Beverly could be anywhere within the range of Cleveland." He called in the State Highway Department and the county engineers to join the melancholy search.

Like a deadly plague, fear began to spread quietly and inevitably through the Linnet Avenue neighborhood. Youngsters continued to play at Hal-loran Park as they always had, but now small groups of mothers stood off to the side anxiously monitoring the activities of their children. Some of the concerned parents reported that they had occasionally seen "bums" in the playground. A number recalled having seen Beverly at the show on the night she disappeared. None had the slightest idea what had happened to her, but they were making sure the same thing

Neighbors watch silently as firemen with flashlights search the culvert south of Thrush Avenue in the early evening of August 27. *Cleveland Press* Archives, Cleveland State University.

did not happen to their children. After 6:00 P.M., the *Plain Dealer* reported on August 28, the playground hosted almost as many parents as kids, and a number of children deserted the park to play in their front yards. Halloran Park also swarmed with police. At first the children responded with excitement to all the questions from adult authority figures. But it eventually began to sink in that something terrible had happened to their friend and classmate, and their faces began to cloud over with a vacant apprehension that mirrored the fear in the eyes of their watchful parents. When darkness started to settle around 8:00 P.M., mothers began hustling the remaining stragglers away from Halloran toward the safety of their own houses. By the time night closed in completely, all the front doors that lined Linnet Avenue had been closed and securely locked; both park and street stretched into the gloom—silent, dark, and deserted.

As night approached, a contingent of firemen in hip boots and armed with flashlights moved cautiously down the slopes of the nearby culvert at West 117 and Thrush to search the bottom. A crowd of close to two thousand—neighborhood fathers, mothers, children—gathered on the rim and stared silently as the firemen moved carefully and deliberately through the bottom of the relatively shallow gorge. In grim, almost dread fascination, the huge throng of onlookers watched—sometimes hoping that searchers would not find anything, occasionally wishing they would. In stark contrast to the hushed vigil at Thrush, noisy, almost rowdy crowds began to gather in front of the Potts home. Since the night of Saturday, August 25, lines of cars filled with curiosity seekers had driven by to get a look at the house; now *Press* staff writer Ben Marino watched the evolving scene in stunned disbelief. Though among the most thorough and thoughtful of reporters, he remained a sensitive, philosophical man who loved to sing Italian songs and avoided the truck-driver vocabulary employed so freely by his cynical, hard-bitten colleagues. He did not mix easily with his fellow reporters at Louis Seltzer's *Press;* the do-and-say-anything-in-the-name-of-a-good-story philosophy was simply not his style. "Linnet Ave. was like a carnival midway last night as curious hundreds swelled to thousands, strolling, driving, choking the narrow street, pushing, elbowing for a glance at the heart-break home of Beverly Potts," he fumed on the *Press*'s front page the next day. "There was everything but the hotdog stands. And it was not a pretty sight," he

Part of the unruly crowd that gathered in front of the Potts home on the night of August 27. *Cleveland Press* Archives, Cleveland State University.

Beverly's older sister, Anita. Twelve at the time of Beverly's birth, Anita Potts was twenty-two when her sister vanished. This photograph is part of a series taken by the *Press* and intended for use in conjunction with reporter Ben Marino's article praising Anita's running of the Pottses' household in the immediate aftermath of her sister's disappearance. Though clearly posed, this shot seems considerably less staged than others in the group. When she learned this particular picture would appear in this book, Anita quipped, "Well, at least it isn't the one of me hanging up the laundry." *Cleveland Press* Archives, Cleveland State University.

declared in disgust. On the normally quiet street, every house blazed with lights; policeman shouted at drivers trying to inch their way through the milling crowds that, at their height, numbered an estimated two thousand people. "Parents brought children," Marino raged. "Teen-agers brought girls. It was like a date. Instead of going to a show, they came to this gloomy house where tragedy struck."

Inside, the Potts family had retreated to the kitchen, the farthest point in the house from the circus on the street. Robert Potts continued to chain-smoke. "This can't be happening to us—but it is," he kept repeating to *Press* reporters. Both he and Anita sometimes accompanied searchers on their rounds just to keep busy, to give themselves something more to do than simply wait. Anita Potts continued to emerge as the heroine of the household. A high achiever during her entire student career, she had graduated from high school and had gone on to Notre Dame College for Women in 1947. Thanks to special arrangements made through the college, Anita had lived and worked part-time at Rainbow Children's Hospital in South Euclid while taking classes. After graduation in June 1951, she had moved back to Linnet Avenue and accepted a job as a general clerk at the National Cash Register Company, on Euclid Avenue. Now she kept the coffee brewing in the Potts home for visitors, managed to find a cigarette for anyone who had run out, kept the front rooms neat, and answered the constantly ringing telephone. "If Anita Potts has shed any tears or expressed any fears for Beverly, they have been seen or heard only by members of her family," Marino wrote on August 29. "To the world at large she is nerveless."

Her mother, Elizabeth, however—deprived of sleep, wracked by worry—continued to sink into deep despair. Observers noticed that she seemed to be crying softly virtually all the time. She fretted over the fact that Beverly had not been dressed for cold nights and worried that her daughter was not being properly fed or kept warm. Both her husband and daughter worried about her health. "As long as I don't know anything, I am going to believe that Beverly is all right and will come back to us," she assured the *Press* on August 27. "I would be all right if the back door slammed, and I heard Beverly shout, 'Hi, ma,'" she remarked wistfully. At times, however, hidden reserves of strength flickered briefly. "I slept last night," she matter-of-factly told the *Press* on August 28. "There may come a time for hysterics—but not now."

NOTES

Doris O'Donnell Beaufait provided the wonderful description of her friend and colleague *Press* staff writer Ben Marino.

$\mathcal{A}$ $\mathcal{T}rickle$ of $\mathcal{S}uspects$

It is my prayer that through the combined efforts of everyone we
will be able to return Beverly Potts to her parents and her home.
Mayor Thomas A. Burke, in an evening radio appeal

The most striking feature about Tuesday's newspaper coverage was that
so little of the information was actually new.

For the first time since the investigation began, papers reported that
police were actually holding a couple of men for questioning. Authorities had picked up a forty-two-year-old machinist who had hailed a taxi
downtown and asked to be driven to Halloran Park. In a startlingly similar
incident, a fifty-one-year-old Great Lakes sailor had gotten into a cab
with several bags of candy that, according to the cabbie, he wanted to
distribute to the children playing at Halloran. Authorities were also looking for a third suspect, a tall, ruddy-complexioned man who had been
seen in a downtown department store in the company of a girl who
answered Beverly's description. It didn't take much to attract the suspicious attention of the authorities. That police would react so decisively
to such slender leads demonstrates, perhaps better than anything else,
how desperate they were becoming as the unsuccessful hunt entered its
fourth day.

Suddenly, every piece of discarded clothing and every suspicious-look-
ing object came under official scrutiny. Scientific experts examined a
charred baseball bat for blood stains, but tests proved negative. A pair of
blue jeans and a blue jacket, similar to what Beverly had been wearing
Friday night, turned up at Edgewater Park, but her parents didn't think
the articles of clothing were hers. A shirt found by three boys in a wooded

area near West 140 Street and Victory Boulevard turned out to be splattered with paint rather than blood.

A psychic contacted Cleveland police on Tuesday, August 28. Back in 1932, at the time of the Lindbergh kidnapping, he related, he had had a vision of a man he later recognized as Bruno Hauptmann climbing a ladder leaning against the Lindbergh residence. At the time, however, he had kept his visions to himself. Now he had had a similar experience concerning Beverly Potts, and this time he was not about to repeat his twenty-year-old mistake by keeping silent. Beverly, he assured police, had been killed by a black man, and her body could be found in one of the boxcars in the Linndale railroad yards. Like so many other potential leads in the Potts case, this tantalizing—if somewhat bizarre—tip is left dangling. Police did inspect the Linndale railroad yards carefully, but none of the surviving documents makes it clear whether or not this psychic tip sent them back for another look at the deserted boxcars.

Several local stations carried Mayor Thomas Burke's evening radio plea to the public simultaneously, but because it occurred in the evening, the *Plain Dealer* was the only daily newspaper in the city to report on it. Burke thanked "every arm of your city government" for working far beyond the call of duty in the ever-widening search for the missing little girl. "As mayor of Cleveland I ask tonight that all citizens join in this search. I ask that they look around old buildings, back yards of vacant houses; that they look around buildings under construction, not only in the neighborhood where this young girl lived but all over the city." As if the number of tips flooding in to the police department had not already reached staggering, virtually unmanageable proportions, he gave the public the detective bureau's phone number—MAine 1–1270—and urged city residents to report any bit of information, "trivial as it may seem."

The police and city papers needed a recent photograph of the missing girl to push the investigation forward. The Potts family dutifully turned over what they considered to be the best picture ever taken of Beverly. Unfortunately, the photo, though recent, dated from the days when she wore her hair long and showed her in a dress. *Press* artist Jim Herron, therefore, altered the picture to reflect both her current personal appearance and the clothes she had been wearing on the night of August 24.

After the appalling spectacle in front of the Potts home the previous night, Linnet Avenue residents petitioned police to block off the street.

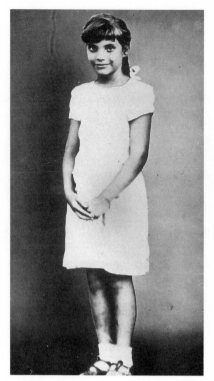 

At left: A photo of Beverly given to Cleveland police by the Potts family. They judged it one of the best pictures ever taken of the missing child. Clearly, the image of Beverly has been cut from a larger photograph and placed on a blank background. The Cleveland Police Department. At right: The same photograph as altered by *Press* artist Jim Herron to reflect Beverly's physical appearance and attire the night of August 24, 1951. *Cleveland Press* Archives, Cleveland State University.

Accordingly, patrolman Charles J. Vrana put up traffic barriers at both ends of the block at West 117 and Bosworth. At least the appearance of normality could return to the once quiet neighborhood. Beverly's uncle William Potts wondered if she could have been abducted by a woman—a possibility that perhaps would explain why there had apparently been no outcry. "We warned her constantly about talking with strange men," Robert Potts told the *Press*. "But we never thought to warn her against women."

Authorities routinely withhold bits of information from the public during a high-profile investigation for a variety of reasons, among them, to avoid tipping off potential suspects and to keep secret pertinent details that can be used to screen out crackpot confessions. But on Wednesday,

August 29, Cleveland police announced a major break in the case. After the paucity of published information the day before, they revealed that they now had a prime suspect in the Potts disappearance—one they had been tracking since Saturday. POLICE CALL WEST SIDER "BEST SUSPECT," trumpeted the headline to Russell Faist's front-page story in the *Cleveland News* that evening; NEW SUSPECT NABBED IN MISSING CHILD CASE, proclaimed the *Press* on page one. (Timing can be everything in journalistic readership wars; the *Plain Dealer* had to wait until the next morning to cover the story.)

A twenty-six-year-old man, known in the newspapers only as "Bill," became the first in a surprisingly short list of bizarre lowlifes actually considered viable suspects by the police. (Police reports identify him as William R. Slates.) He had been among the known West Side sex offenders authorities began tracking down almost immediately after Beverly's disappearance. "This lead is the most promising we have had so far," the usually cautious James McArthur told the *Press*, and, indeed, the suspect's squalid history and current lifestyle made him a plausible candidate in the case. The man had been arrested and placed on a year's probation in March 1949 for making advances toward an eight-year-old girl in a movie theater while on furlough from the army. At the time, county psychiatrist Royal Grossman had, according to the *News*, diagnosed the young offender as an "inadequate personality, mildly neurotic," clearly in need of prolonged "psycho therapy treatment." Military authorities had promptly court-martialed the apparent deviant and tossed him out of the service with a dishonorable discharge. Neighbors called him a ne'er-do-well. As far as the police were concerned, he was a "mental case" and "motorcycle addict" who had lived with his widowed mother close to Halloran Park on West 116 Street since 1950, couldn't hold a job for more than a couple of weeks, brought a constant stream of young girls to his mother's house, and was currently "going steady" with a seventeen-year-old telephone operator. According to neighbors, the man had suddenly locked up the house—his mother was vacationing in Virginia for two weeks—and vanished the Sunday after Beverly's disappearance. Police subsequently had placed the house under surveillance, and when they later raided and ransacked it, they reportedly found a 25-calibre automatic and a loaded clip in a bureau drawer.

For some strange reason never adequately explained, "Bill" had borrowed a friend's car on Sunday and driven down to Columbus, where he took up temporary residence in a hotel. Police had traced him through

Police examine "Bill's" car in Columbus, Ohio. *Cleveland Press* Archives, Cleveland State University.

a telephone call placed to his teenage girl friend. Columbus police placed the mysterious suspect under arrest at 2:00 P.M. on August 29 and passed him into the custody of detectives Vincent Morrow and Patrick Gereau. He turned out to be quite a con man. He explained and defended his actions of the past few days with such a stream of glib jabber that police—operating on the assumption that Beverly had most likely been lured away by such a fast and persuasive talker—ironically became more convinced of his guilt. His plight became even more serious when Dale Smallwood and Frazer Jenkins, two of his buddies snared by the authorities at the same time, offered varying and conflicting accounts of the suspect's actions on the night of August 24. "Bill" did not do particularly well when police subjected him to a lie-detector test, but whatever case they may have thought they had against him collapsed when his teenage amour came forward and confirmed that he had been making out with her in a car at Edgewater Park when Beverly Potts disappeared. Apparently, authorities accepted her story, for there is no surviving documentation, either in the press or the police files, that their investigation into "Bill" and his questionable affairs continued.

. . .

The residents of Linnet Avenue continued to live under a state of siege, and authorities placed the Potts home under virtual quarantine. Though food from the neighbors continued to pour into the house, borne on a flood of goodwill and heartfelt sympathy, the Pottses' neighbors were torn between their desire to offer whatever help they could and their recognition that the family needed a little breathing space. Even the detectives working on the case went to the house only when it was absolutely necessary. Generally, they came in the early, predawn hours when the street was at its most quiet, but no matter what time they arrived, someone in the house was up and about. With the family's permission, police intercepted, opened, and screened all their incoming mail before it was delivered to the house by detective sergeant Robert Slusser. The constant waves of telephone calls abated when the phone company disconnected the family's number. The newspaper reporters from Cleveland's three dailies still held their increasingly useless vigils on the Cassano front porch across from the Potts house. "Seltzer kept sending his men out to the house every day," former *News* reporter Doris O'Donnell Beaufait says, "so we all had to keep going out there too." The police barricades slowed the volume of automobile traffic cruising by the Potts residence, but many of the morbidly determined simply moved them out of the way. The huge crowds of the previous days began to dwindle, but pedestrian traffic continued to pick up as night closed in. Isolated inside their small house, the Potts family continued to receive the support of sympathetic neighbors. One man drove the streets searching for signs of the missing child every evening when he got off work; someone else would make sure the Pottses' lawn was mowed. Neighbors brought so much food to the house that some of it had to be given away.

In the field the hunt for Beverly continued, but the heart had gone out of it. Now entering its fifth day, the massive effort, involving so many individuals and organizations—both public and private—had turned up nothing. Still, calling off the search was not an option; it simply had to go on. The constant waves of rumors that Beverly had been found either alive or dead compromised the effort, since authorities had to spend so much time checking out such leads, no matter how wild or improbable. At the detective bureau, McArthur—who had again gone sleepless, though for how long is unclear—continued to direct the investigation. He gave some thought to using bloodhounds to trace

Beverly's movements, but abandoned the notion when experts insisted the dogs would be of little use in heavily traveled areas. He similarly jettisoned an idea to publicly summon every attendee at the Showagon performance because too many people who weren't at Halloran that night might show up as well, out of curiosity. McArthur did, however, mail copies of Beverly's picture to every police department within a several-hundred-mile radius of Cleveland and made sure that every city patrol car and most of those in the suburbs carried the little girl's photograph. Slusser led an army of fifty Boy Scouts through the empty fields southwest of the city, while McArthur and several hundred city employees explored other desolate areas. Captain Richard R. Wagner took thirty-five men from the Cleveland Police Academy to the Brooklyn Heights area near Schaaf Road; the next day, he supervised a contingent of Brook Park police and men from the academy in a sweep around Cleveland Hopkins Airport. Mounted patrolmen rode west along the Erie shore beginning at West 58. James Hoy, chief of the Metropolitan Park police, directed an army of his men—on horseback, on motorcycles, and on foot—through every ravine in the vast park system and drafted twenty-six area lifeguards to help.

On Wednesday events took a decidedly darker turn. Mail carrier Fred Manheim found a frightening letter addressed to Burke in the collection box at East 93 and St. Clair. Signed "Unknown," the message stated that Beverly Potts had been kidnapped, sexually assaulted, and murdered; her abductor and killer had then thrown her body into Lake Erie at East 71. McArthur thought the letter was an exceptionally cruel hoax, so he declined the proffered services of a professional diver. But authorities could not afford to take the disturbing letter too lightly, so McArthur checked with Lester Adelson of the coroner's office to learn how long a child's body might remain submerged before it would rise to the surface, and he asked the Coast Guard to comb every inch of the lake from the city of Lorain in the west to that of Fairport Harbor in the east.

For four days published and broadcast descriptions of Beverly Potts had operated on the assumption that she might be wandering the city somewhere and, therefore, had focused on what she had been wearing on the night of August 24. Now, on the fifth day, more intimate details crept into those descriptions—the sort of things that could only be checked if a body were to be found: "birthmark one-half inch in diameter on the back of left foot: upper and lower molars have silver fillings . . . brand name on shoes, 'Karrybrooke Sportshoes': shoes resoled and heeled: white cotton undershirt with tag 'Honey Lane': bright red cotton panties with elastic around waist but not around legs . . . blue girls' jeans, zipper on side, size 14 or 16, no tag: red-colored sports shirt, no label: navy blue poplin jacket, both pockets torn, no label." McArthur made sure the amended melancholy description was broadcast six times a day over the county's police network.

NOTES

"Bill's" story was carried by all three Cleveland's dailies. Police reports deal with this part of the investigation in enormous detail, but the official coverage is dispersed among several different stapled packets of documents (making continuity an almost insurmountable problem), and, though copies are curiously not kept together, some of the reports are duplicated.

Seltzer Turns Up the Hysteria

WHY CHILDREN DISAPPEAR!
part of the headline for a page-one story in the Press

If jittery and worried Clevelanders still wondered how a young girl could disappear so completely from a neat, safe West Side neighborhood, the *Press* told them why: 1000 SEX OFFENDERS ARE FREE IN CITY screamed the headline.

"There is a pool of 1037 potential suspects in the Beverly Potts disappearance," the unsigned article began. "Two hundred of them are persons who have been charged with felonious assault or rape." After the brutal shock of its attention-grabbing opening, the piece actually settled into a detailed, yet concise summary of how local authorities kept track of all known sex offenders in the city. To a twenty-first-century reader familiar with contemporary laws and procedures governing known sexual predators and pedophiles in society, the sophistication of police record-keeping methods fifty years ago will probably come as a distinct surprise. In addition to cataloguing their vital statistics and residences, authorities classified all molesters and anyone else arrested in a sex case by gender of preferred victims and by the threat posed to society—in other words, by whether the perpetrator was an actual predator or merely a peeping Tom. Along with providing such reassuring information, however, the *Press* article railed at purported weaknesses in the legal system in a manner designed to make modern civil-rights advocates flinch. And James McArthur grumbled, "I'm not a medical man—but I think a lot more of these persons should be locked up."

As leads continued to dwindle, all three daily papers took the opportunity to editorialize about the implications of Beverly Potts's disappearance and the lessons to be learned from it. The most thoughtful of these warnings came from the *Plain Dealer* on August 28. In an article titled "Parents Advised to Warn Children," the paper listed precautions that parents could take to protect youngsters suggested by four different workers in the field: Marjorie H. Boggs (director of casework for the Family Service Association), Lieutenant Joseph T. Creagan (police juvenile bureau), Lieutenant Helen Hollmer (policewoman's bureau), and Mark C. Schinnerer (superintendent of schools). The experts stressed the importance of keeping strict tabs on children's activities and educating them to the dangers posed by strangers. The bottom line, however, was that "this is an individual problem and the responsibility of parents." A *News* editorial on the same day covered similar ground but went on to advocate greater attention to molestation cases from the courts, stricter parole supervision, and improved treatment facilities for offenders at area hospitals. "The greatest tragedy of all," concluded the writer, "is this: That such crimes must occur before the intelligent people of this community, and the state, act to prevent them."

Authorities had what they felt were two new viable suspects. The first was a fifty-six-year-old railroad worker who had been in and out of the courts over a period of years on a variety of molestation allegations and who lived near Halloran Park. He wound up in jail because he owned a dark car and police had judged him "evasive" when they first questioned him. When Detective Samuel A. Mears showed the man's picture to several of Beverly's schoolmates, they identified him as someone who "hung around" Halloran Park. Police subjected the man to two lie-detector tests, at least one of them conducted by David L. Cowles, longtime head of the police scientific bureau and one-time associate and confidant of Cleveland's former safety director, Eliot Ness. Sometimes seemingly evasive and often very nervous, the suspect insisted he had been home on the night of August 24 and had had absolutely nothing to do with Beverly Potts's disappearance. In spite of what McArthur termed the man's "nervous reaction to pertinent questions," police could find no major flaws in his story. When the man's wife substantiated his alibi, authorities turned him loose.

The second suspect, identified only as a thirty-seven-year-old man, brought with him a tale sufficiently convoluted and strange to impress the most jaded of soap-opera writers. Sergeant Thomas E. Devries and Detective Milo Sebek of the Cleveland police force checked out an abandoned car east of the city in North Randall at the intersection of Warrensville Center and Miles Roads, a vehicle nearby residents insisted had been sitting there for two or three days. Inside the suspicious auto, Devries and Sebek discovered a ripped pair of women's pedal pushers, a pair of men's underwear (both apparently bloodstained), a washcloth, a magazine, and the August 25 edition of the *News.*

Police traced the derelict vehicle to a rental agency that, in turn, linked it to an extremely agitated man who had been so desperate for a car on the Friday night Beverly Potts vanished that he was willing to accept a truck. The still unidentified suspect had then wooed a twenty-nine-year-old woman with a promise of marriage and a trip to West Virginia. After a brief stopover in Warren, Ohio, the couple finally landed in Pittsburgh, where the mysterious man suddenly deserted his confused would-be bride, headed back to Cleveland, and abandoned the car where police found it a couple days later. Not only had the man recently worked as a painter on houses in the vicinity of the Potts home, his behavior struck police as utterly inexplicable. Among other things, he was already married. McArthur adamantly insisted to the *Plain Dealer* on August 31 that the suspect must be interrogated. "Why was he in such a hurry to rent a car?" he fumed. "Why did a married man want to run away to marry again? Why did he abandon the woman in Pittsburgh?" And most importantly, "Did anything the man did Friday [August 24, the night Beverly vanished] have bearing on his actions the next day?" Whether McArthur ever got any answers to his questions remains a mystery; there are no further references to the bizarre painter in the Cleveland press.

Louis Seltzer now really outdid himself. "We Must Stay Aroused to This Peril," he warned in the title of a signed, boxed, front-page editorial in the *Press* on Friday, August 31. "The very awfulness of it makes strong men shudder," he wrote. "Three innocent little girls—in three years. Shelia Ann Tuley [brutally stabbed to death in 1948]. And Gail Ann Michell [abducted but returned in May 1951]. Now Beverly Potts." Seltzer insisted that the outrage such cases routinely engendered must not be allowed to dissipate; rather, it should be effectively channeled into "a program to set up facilities for getting these human menaces where society can be protected against them and something intelligent done

Louis B. Seltzer, the powerful editor of the *Cleveland Press*. Seltzer was one of the city's kingmakers and enjoyed access to innumerable levers of local power. No doubt because his paper had cosponsored the Showagon performance from which Beverly had so mysteriously vanished, he kept the poignant story on the front pages for weeks. The *Press*'s often lurid treatment of the Potts disappearance would turn the missing ten-year-old into a Cleveland legend and serve as a warm-up for the paper's heavy-handed and biased coverage of the Shepherd murder case a mere three years later. *Cleveland Press* Archives, Cleveland State University.

about them." Though no one could argue with the main thrust of his appeal, Seltzer compromised his call to action by a total lack of specifics and crippled it completely with an overly sensational, rabble-rousing rhetoric more appropriate for tabloids and sleazy politicians. "All the while a thousand potential molesters—and killers—of innocent little children, especially innocent little girls, roaming the streets. Infesting the neighborhoods. Luring children with candy, money, promises. Constantly endangering happy, playing, carefree children." His lurid depiction of a world filled with looming dangers for the young seems designed to terrify rather than warn or enlighten. "But in the meantime, every day, every month, every year, some innocent child is molested by these sex offenders, perverts and mentally sick who roam around outside of institutions—mingling every day with their potential prey."

. . .

Once again, Cleveland police thought they had a major break in the case. Authorities hauled in three new suspects for questioning, an unsavory threesome the *Press* branded "a 19-year-old hot rod queen and two of her speed-crazy boy friends." The trio had come to McArthur's attention through nineteen-year-old Francis Patacca—also dubbed by the *News* as "a hot rodder"—and his wife, Cherie. After an intense, two-hour grilling, the pair relayed a story to the cautious, ever-dubious James McArthur that could have been pulled from the pages of a cheap pulp-fiction novel. According to Patacca, on the night of Beverly's disappearance, Clevelander Barbara Saunders, the blonde "hot rod queen," had loaned her 1940 Chevrolet coupe to nineteen-year-old Don Croft (known as Crazy Don, according to police reports) of Olmsted Falls, Ohio, and eighteen-year-old Russell Veit. Patacca further alleged that the duo phoned her later in the evening and told her that they had abandoned her car in the woods after having had an accident on West 117 Street and warned her not to go near it because it was "hot." As a further warning to Saunders to keep silent, the pair allegedly beat up her boyfriend. (The boyfriend was identified as Russell Veit's brother, Carl, in a memo from Forest Allan in the *Press* files, but there is obvious confusion as to which brother did what.) According to the *Press*, on August 31, when the nineteen-year-old girl retrieved her auto the next day, she reportedly found blood on the bumper (which she immediately wiped off) and a torn piece of cloth on the grill—rumors McArthur dismissed as unverified. Supposedly, her two friends admitted to Saunders that they had struck a little girl on West 117, tossed her body into the car, and later buried it a wooded area of Brook Park Village, close to the "hot rod queen's" home. Could Saunders's car be the black coupe with two young men inside that several park visitors reportedly saw Beverly standing near at the close of the show in Halloran on August 24? (Subsequently, yet another police dragnet snared several other alleged hot-rod enthusiasts for questioning.)

Granted, there is no clear indication in the reporting as to when this supposed hit-and-run took place, but how could anything remotely similar to what Croft and Veit allegedly described to Saunders have happened on such a street as heavily traveled as West 117, next to a playground overflowing with visitors, without anyone seeing anything? Yet the press did not question the story, nor, apparently, did the police. The press apparently found Patacca's story so compellingly lurid that they printed every detail without questioning any of it. And the police seem to have accepted it as well, at least in part. In the early morning darkness of August 31, McArthur and several squads of police officers headed for the designated area armed with picks, shovels, and lanterns. They dug by lantern light for several hours in the lonely area looking for a shallow grave but found nothing. Undaunted, they turned their attention to Saunders's house, but similarly came up empty. An examination of the girl's car turned up several blonde hairs caught in a door hinge that police believed could have been Beverly's.

Saunders and the two male youths vehemently denied Patacca's entire story. Croft insisted he had been in Michigan on the night of August 24, and the eighteen-year-old Russell Veit said he had been on a date. Under intense police questioning, nineteen-year-old Saunders veered from defiance to nervousness to outraged anger. The *Press* even described her as "spunky" on August 31. When authorities confronted her with Francis Patacca (who also worked at Asbestos Products Company on Detroit with Saunders), the girl, according to the *Press*, screamed at him, "You got me into this." Both the *Press* and the *News* carried this lurid tale of accident, threats, and deception. Accuser and accused, however, remained adamant: Patacca, the hot-rodder turned informant, stuck by his story, and Saunders insisted it was all a lie. In spite of all the high drama, nothing significant emerged from this web of intrigue; the next day, police released the hot-rod trio and the suspicious car. Thus the gang of hot-rodders rounded up by Cleveland police vanished from the Beverly Potts investigation, never to reappear. Unfortunately, any further reference, official or otherwise, to the tell-tale blonde hairs allegedly found on the bumper of Saunders's car has similarly disappeared.

A new major player had unobtrusively made his entrance on the scene: chief of homicide David E. Kerr had been present during the interrogation of the hot-rod threesome. The press noted his presence but failed to grasp its significance. Opinions both popular and official may have come to the conclusion that Beverly Potts was dead, but there was no body. And, traditionally, the homicide unit has been extremely reluctant to interest itself in a case unless there is a corpse. Here, however, there was no clear proof there had even been a murder. At best, police had uncovered a possible hit-and-run incident—hardly the sort of thing to interest someone as high on the ladder of authority as the chief of homicide. Why was Kerr even present? "He was either injected into the investigation by someone or he injected himself," reasons retired Cleveland Police commander Robert Cermak. That someone who "injected" Kerr into

David E. Kerr. The head of homicide was one of the most visible and powerful men in the Cleveland Police Department. The photograph dates from 1948 and was probably taken in conjunction with the high profile murder of eight-year-old Shelia Ann Tuley. Photo: The *Plain Dealer* Collection, Cleveland Public Library.

the case was probably police chief George Matowitz, responding to additional pressure from *Press* editor Louis Seltzer. Kerr was McArthur's exact opposite. Where the chief of detectives was a soft-spoken, cautious, and intense investigator, the chief of homicide was a gregarious, flamboyant, larger-than-life personality. He often held court at the Theatrical (a popular bar and restaurant) in downtown Cleveland, and newspaper reporters in need of a good tip could always count on David Kerr. "The only cop I knew who wore blue suede shoes," recalls former reporter Doris O'Donnell Beaufait with an affectionate laugh. "A legend in his own mind," quips a near contemporary colleague with a wry smile. "One of the most powerful men in the department, more powerful than some politicians," observes Detective Robert Wolf. For better or worse, this odd couple, Kerr and McArthur, would be inseparably linked in the Beverly Potts investigation until McArthur retired from the department in 1957.

In the ensuing months, the stream of official paperwork on the investigation swelled to a flood. The pool of potential suspects grew wider; the tips to which police responded grew less and less promising. But the numbing routine of searching and checking dragged on. Over and over again, police reports closed with the same frustrating coda. "Nothing of value pertaining to this case." "On the basis of the above information we are un-able [*sic*] to connect . . . with the dis-appearance [*sic*] of Beverly Potts." "We are satisfied that the above subject was not in any way connected with the disappearance of Beverly Potts." "From our investigation we are satisfied there is no connection with the Potts girl." "Unable to learn anything that would be of any value to us with this investigation at this time." "Up to this time we have found no information that would lead in any manner in locating the above missing child."

"Tragedy, like war, makes people pull together," wrote *Press* reporter Ben Marino on Friday, August 31. "That is the way it has been along Linnet Ave. since last Saturday. The whole neighborhood overnight assumed a single purpose: To do anything possible to help the parents of Beverly

A Cleveland Police circular alerting the public to and requesting information about missing Beverly Potts. The Cleveland Police Historical Society Museum.

O YEAR OLD-BEVERLY POTTS-MISSING

DESCRIPTION OF BEVERLY POTTS, 11304 LINNET AVE., CLEVELAND, OHIO
MISSING SINCE 9:30 P.M., AUG. 24, 1951

WHITE FEMALE - 10 YEARS OF AGE - HEIGHT - 4'11" - WEIGHT - 90
POUNDS. HAS LIGHT COMPLEXION - BLUE EYES, SPACED WIDE APART,
SMALL SCAR OVER LEFT EYEBROW - DARK BLOND HAIR, REPORTED TO BE
CUT IN MEDIUM LENGTH BOB, WITH BANGS AND ALSO REPORTED TO BE
THICK. ORDINARY VACCINATION MARK UPPER LEFT ARM. BIRTH MARK,
KIDNEY SHAPED, APPROXIMATELY 1" LONG AND 3/8" WIDE ON INSTEP OF
FOOT - NOT KNOWN WHICH FOOT.

WEARING FOLLOWING CLOTHING

BROWN LOAFER SHOES, SIZE 5 OR 5½ - BRAND NAME, "KARRYBROOKE"
SPORT SHOES; SAME HAVING BEEN RE-SOLED AND HEALED. WHITE-
COTTON UNDERSHIRT WITH TAG, "HONEY LANE" ON SAME. BRIGHT RED
COTTON PANTIES WITH ELASTIC AROUND WAIST BUT NONE AROUND LEGS.
NO TAGS ON PANTIES. PLAIN GREEN SOCKS. BLUE GIRL'S JEANS -
ZIPPER ON SIDE - SIZE 14 OR 16 - NO TAGS. RED COLORED SPORT
SHIRT - NO LABEL, TURTLE NECK STYLE. NAVY BLUE POPLIN JACKET
WITH BOTH POCKETS TORN - NO LABEL. BARE HEADED. HAD TWO METAL
CLASPS IN HAIR THAT HAD BROWN PLASTIC COVERS ON SAME. MAY BE
WEARING A RING, YELLOW GOLD, SIMILAR TO WEDDING RING HAVING
SPACE FOR SEVEN OR EIGHT SMALL STONES NOW ALL MISSING. COULD
PASS FOR TWELVE (12) YEARS OF AGE....

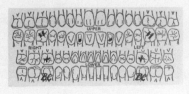

6	2 OCCLUSAL ALLOYS
6	2 OCCLUSAL ALLOYS
2	LINGUAL PIT ALLOY
2	LINGUAL PIT ALLOY
6	CEMENT BASE & ALLOY
6	CEMENT BASE & ALLOY

LIBERAL REWARD FOR LOCATING THIS PERSON DEAD OR ALIVE
NOTIFY GEO. J. MATOWITZ, CHIEF OF POLICE, CLEVELAND 14, OHIO

A homey touch amid the unfolding tragedy. The neighbor ladies of Linnet Avenue serve lunch to some of the reporters and photographers who had staked out the Potts residence. From left to right: *News* writer Russell Faist, Helen Eiben, an unidentified *Press* photographer, Ann Cossano, the *Press*'s top police reporter Forest Allen, unidentified, and *News* photographer Jerry Horton. This impromptu meal took place on the Cossano front porch almost directly across the street from the Potts home. *Cleveland Press* Archives, Cleveland State University.

Potts. There isn't any organization, no committees, no paper work. Instead, there are a lot of folks who think up things to do and go do them." Earlier in the week, he had watched with something approaching horror the ugly circus in front of the Potts home, but now he noted the small, heartfelt acts of generosity by the Linnet Avenue residents; even a gesture as simple as a neighbor passing a carton of cigarettes to Robert Potts won his approval. "As you spend day after day in the neighborhood, you have a feeling that here is a reservoir of strength for the household overtaken by tragedy. Whatever its outcome, the Potts family does not face it alone. Whoever took Beverly away took on not just a family, but a neighborhood." At St. Philip and James Church on Bosworth Road, a reporter from the *News* watched quietly while three of Beverly's playmates—Leonard Eiben, Karen Ann Kilbane, and Linda Sloan—offered their simple prayers for their friend's return. "We looked all over for her and now all we can do is pray," they volunteered softly. "Please bring Beverly home safe."

NOTES

The odyssey of the unidentified fifty-six-year-old suspect while in the custody of the police again demonstrates the level of confusion that clouds newspaper coverage of the case. One report alleges that he flunked a pair of lie-detector tests; another insists he was released a few days later when he successfully passed such an examination. Newspaper accounts also refer to a fifty-four-year-old suspect. Neither of them was identified by name in the press, and I could not locate any police reports that would untangle the situation. While these men do seem to be two entirely different individuals, it is tempting to think that some of the seeming discrepancies in the reporting could be due to the two men becoming confused with each other.

There is even greater confusion over the Patacca-Saunders-Croft-Veit hot-rod incident. Though extensive, the press coverage remains difficult to follow since no names are used. Instead, the reader is left to wallow in a confusing sea of pronouns and other signifiers. The surviving police reports provide the names of everyone involved, but the files are regrettably incomplete.

Ben Marino's coverage of the Linnet Avenue neighborhood's response to the Potts family tragedy appeared in the August 30 issue of the *Press;* the brief note about the prayers of Beverly's three friends was printed in the August 31 edition of the *News.*

PART TWO

Ripples in the Pond: Becoming a Legend

False Leads and Weary Frustration

Cleveland News staff writer Howard Beaufait began September with a melancholy assessment of the Potts case in an article, "Crime Pattern Stacks Against Missing Child." He wrote, "And I am certain of only one thing, Beverly Potts will not be returned to her home alive." Beaufait was a highly respected senior member of the *News* staff; an inductee into the Cleveland Journalism Hall of Fame, he had covered the Kingsbury Run murders in the 1930s and had recently contributed to the book *Cleveland Murders*. In his reflective piece, combining both editorial comment and personal memoir, he revisited the events of the previous week, catalogued the divisions in the army of searchers, touched briefly on the pain in the Potts household, and commented on the seeming hopelessness of the situation—all of which led him to his grim conclusion that Beverly Potts was dead. On September 13 *News* reporter Harry Christianson eloquently described his three weeks of grinding frustration working on the Potts story—an exhausting personal odyssey of fruitless searches through the wild areas close to Halloran Park and an endless parade of dead-end leads and tips, including one that Beverly had once carved her initials into one of the park's wooden benches. During the two weeks separating these two pieces, the desperate search for any clues in the girl's disappearance continued—driven by a combination of the still intense media coverage, sustained public interest, and personal dedication on the part of authorities. Under normal circumstances, police officers changed shifts every thirty days, but now they began to ignore that routine. After a nonstop, thirty-five hour stint on the job, James McArthur finally took a brief rest around September 1. On September 4, a physician ordered the exhausted chief of detectives, now battling a cold, to bed; two days later, he was back in the field

leading the troops. Reports of Beverly sightings all over the city continued to trickle into authorities. The Press Club devoted its weekly WHK
broadcast to the Potts mystery and to what could be done to prevent
future abductions. Halloran Park became a local magnet attracting both
children and adults—dubbed amateur sleuths by the *Plain Dealer*—who
hung around the "crime scene" soaking up the atmosphere and eagerly
sharing their notions of what might have happened on the night of
August 24 with each other, curious reporters, and the police, who—
under the circumstances—seemed willing to listen to almost anything.
In the Potts household, daily routines gradually returned to normal.
The family began going to bed before midnight; both Robert Potts and
daughter Anita returned to their jobs. The missing child began to slip
gradually from the front pages of city dailies. By midmonth, she would
pass from the press's radar completely—at least for the time being—and
take her first steps into becoming a Cleveland legend.

ECHOES FROM THE PAST

Both the Sheila Ann Tuley murder of 1948 and the recent Gail Ann
Michel abduction were fresh in the minds of Clevelanders, and the obvious parallels between these two cases and the Beverly Potts disappearance got a thorough examination in the press. The grisly death of Sheila
Ann Tuley in 1948 had shocked the city almost four years before the
disappearance of Beverly Potts. Sent on an errand by her father on the
evening of New Year's Day, the child was waylaid and brutally stabbed
to death by a man named Harold Beach. Beach was arrested, tried, and
executed for the crime. The four-month-old case of Gail Ann Michel,
however, ended far less tragically. After having been mysteriously abducted, she was suddenly and just as mysteriously released by her cap-
tor in a downtown department store. Mayor Burke also recalled in the
Press the 1931 murder of six-year-old Marian McLean of Cincinnati.

Reporters also rummaged through old files looking for other cases
that, in some way, paralleled the Potts disappearance. On August 31 the
Press dredged up the 1928 death of twelve-year-old Alice Leonard of
Mayfield Heights, a victim of a hit-and-run incident, whose body lay
undiscovered in a field for two months. More to the point, *News* staff
writer Howard Beaufait eloquently recalled the baffling case of Melvin

Horst of Orrville, Ohio, a city south of Akron, halfway between Cleveland and Columbus, who disappeared without a trace, also in 1928. "Two Ohio children have apparently joined hands today along the path that leads to the moldy archives of unsolved mysteries," he wrote. "They are Beverly Potts of Cleveland and Melvin Horst of Orville. Names of this boy and girl are linked together by the casual and unbelievable circumstances of their disappearances, by thousands of tips and clues that led nowhere, by public concern and bewilderment across the entire state."

A SHORT, PLUMP WOMAN AND A
MAN WITH A POINTED CHIN

A week after the still inexplicable disappearance of her best friend, Patsy Swing, according to the *Press*, had suddenly recalled a pertinent detail about that tragic night; a short, plump woman, holding a small child by the hand, had been standing next to Beverly as the girls watched the show. "I remember she put her hand on Beverly's left shoulder and kind of boosted herself up so she could see the show over Beverly's head," Patsy insisted to the police on September 1. "And I remember her remarking to someone in the crowd that one of her other children was playing in the Showagon cast that night." It would be interesting to know where and how the *Press* picked up these quotes; it all sounds a bit sophisticated and calm for a small child undergoing police questioning. The eleven-year-old girl's revelation, however, was sufficiently strong to send police back out to the Halloran Park–West 117 Street area to begin searching for the mystery woman who, according to McArthur and David Kerr, may not even have realized that she was the last person to see Beverly before she vanished. Subsequently, police picked up a neighborhood woman who had, insisted the *Plain Dealer* on September 2, a "reputation for 'patting' little girls," but Patsy could not identify her as the plump woman nor even recall having ever seen her at Halloran Park.

And so the short, plump woman passed into history and became an integral part of the Beverly Potts legend. But did she ever exist? Or could Patsy have collapsed two separate memories—Beverly alone watching the show and the plump woman with her child somewhere else at some other time in Halloran Park—into a single image? The wording employed by the *Press* to describe the circumstances under which Patsy pulled this detail from her memory provides a chilling clue to the ordeal the poor, frightened child must have endured at the hands of her interrogators, "under intense re-examination by teams of detectives working in relays." And this was "intense" by the standards of the 1950s when the system did not guard the rights of defendants (or witnesses) all that zealously! Though it remains difficult to be absolutely certain, this grueling session apparently did take place at least at the Swing home, thus raising the possibility that her parents were present to offer what support they could. No matter how sensitive they may have been to Patsy's plight, however, none of the detectives "working in relays" had any special training in how to deal with an eleven-year-old child—especially one deeply traumatized by her own inevitable sense of guilt for having left Beverly alone, and by the ferocious media coverage and all the subsequent commotion in front of the Potts home, as well as her own.

I'm not suggesting for a second that Patsy Swing intentionally, or even knowingly, misled authorities, but a terrified little girl undergoing such a horrendous ordeal could easily "remember" something that would satisfy the adult authority figures who had become her tormentors. A few days before, on August 28, Beverly's uncle William Potts had offered police the possibility that Beverly may have been abducted by a woman—explaining, at least in part, why she apparently had not cried out; the notion of a female perpetrator, therefore, was part of the atmosphere hovering around the investigation. Also, if she existed, this mysterious woman—not Patsy herself—would, perhaps, become the "last person to have seen Beverly," thus relieving the beleaguered youngster from at least part of her psychological burden.

Even more ephemeral, a man with a pointed chin was conjured up out of the Halloran Park crowd ten days after Beverly's disappearance on September 4 by Robert Hunt, a twelve-year-old resident of Linnet Avenue who also attended the same school and had been in classes with Beverly. According to this classmate, he and three other boys—all about the same age, two also Linnet Avenue residents—had noticed a short, heavyset, middle-aged man in a light blue suit with a pointed chin (a short, plump man as opposed to a short, plump woman) standing next to Beverly while a ballet dancer performed on stage. Beverly had looked up and smiled at the mysterious figure when he asked, "Wouldn't you like to dance like that?" The four boys had then moved forward closer to the stage, leaving Beverly and the strange man behind.

Caught in a lie. Two of the four boys who reported falsely they had seen Beverly at Halloran Park during the Showagon performance standing next to a short, heavyset man. Though police quickly saw through the ruse and lamented that their time had been wasted on a meaningless lead, the four boys did get their brief moment in the spotlight. From left to right: Ronald Brugeman and Robert Hunt. *Cleveland Press* Archives, Cleveland State University.

Though the ever-skeptical McArthur glowered suspiciously at Hunt's tale, especially since the boys had waited a full ten days to report an incident that seemed so significant, he ordered that photos of known sex offenders be shown to the quartet of young witnesses. Ronald Bruggman, Richard Lutian, and Joseph Arcuri backed up Hunt's account; and the boys' parents explained the delay in coming forward by insisting they were quiet families who simply did not want to get mixed up in such a tragic affair. Two days later on September 6, however, the boys cracked under "severe questioning" by the police and admitted the whole story had been fabricated. A malicious hoax? Perhaps a misguided childish prank or a simple desire to see their names in the papers? It didn't seem to matter much to the authorities; what angered police most, according to the city's dailies, was that they had wasted valuable time pursuing a nonexistent phantom.

AN EVER-WIDENING HUNT AND MORE SUSPECTS

Two more generals joined the massive army of searchers: Captain Arthur V. Roth of the police department's juvenile bureau, described by the *Plain Dealer* on September 1 as an authority on the problems of children, and Detective Samuel A. Mears. Roth returned to the Linnet Avenue neighborhood and reinterviewed the Potts family, thoroughly searched their home, and incurred the wrath of Elizabeth Potts with his request to go through Beverly's toys and room. Mears turned his attention to Louis Agassiz Elementary School, where Beverly had been a pupil. Armed with a list of all fourth, fifth, and sixth graders provided by Principal Harriet Goodyear, the detective began to interview Beverly's schoolmates and their parents on September 1. The next day, he explored every inch of the building and grounds in the company of an unidentified "investigator" from the Cleveland Board of Education. When Cleveland schools opened on Monday, September 10, McArthur formally took over this phase of the investigation as well, leading an impressive—and, no doubt, intimidating—army of detectives and patrolmen to Louis Agassiz Elementary School to systematically question all four hundred students.

In the field, the battalions of searchers, now joined by the National Guard and six hundred more Boy Scouts, spread out into still more unexplored terrain. The discovery of a blond hair on a torn gray blanket hanging on a low tree branch near a "hot-rodder playground–lovers' lane" in Parma and Parma Heights, two of the city's western suburbs, sent more than three dozen auxiliary policemen, Boy Scouts, and police from both Parma and Cleveland combing through the fields and digging in more than a half-dozen spots where the earth seemed recently disturbed. They came up empty-handed save for a piece of newspaper "apparently heavily bloodstained" (according to the *Plain Dealer* on September 3), and two pieces of pink cloth, possibly from the turtlenecked T-shirt Beverly had been wearing on the night of August 24. Searchlights illuminated the valley west of Kamm's Corners, on Cleveland's West Side, and police armed with flashlights explored the valley floor—all because nearby residents reported they had seen two boys toss a suspicious-looking bundle from the Lorain Avenue Bridge. When a Lake Erie fisherman reported to the FBI in Toledo that he had spotted an elderly, white-haired man and a young, blond girl walking through the high weeds on Middle Island (also known as Roscoe's Island) just across the Canadian border in Lake Erie, sixty miles from Cleveland, police combed the small, deserted landmass, as well as Middle Bass Island on the American side of the border. A couple of tips concerning city manholes sent investigators into the murky, filthy depths of Cleveland's sewer system; a report of a "peculiar odor" near the railroad tracks close to Jennings Road and West 14 Street led police, protected by boots and gloves, into the poison-ivy-infected area. A fire department pumper was dispatched to Linndale to drain a ten-foot-deep pond once a New York Central reservoir; an Ohio Bell Telephone crew searched all the underground installations in the area southwest of Halloran. There is a single sheet of paper in the Potts case files—unsigned and undated—containing the text of a directive that apparently went out to all city newspapers. In anticipation of the hunting season that opened on September 22, the directive asked that all hunters watch for anything out of the ordinary as they trekked through the woods and fields. "Most of these hunters will have dogs, and it is in the nature of thins [sic] for dogs to investigate unusual odors and bark. If hunters are alert, it may be that the body of the missing child would be found." Both the police and the Potts family grasped at any new straw that offered even the slightest hope. On the incredibly slim chance that Beverly had somehow managed to get to Euclid Beach (where the Potts family supposedly had planned to picnic on Saturday, August 25, the day after the ten-year-old vanished), Betty Morbito and Anita went to the Erie shore in the company of two city detectives to search the area. (As indicated earlier, Anita Potts does not remember any plans for a family outing on the day after her sister's disappearance, and, even if those plans existed, she considers Euclid Beach a highly unlikely destination.) Similarly, McArthur announced plans to contact all out-of-town Potts family relatives, even while acknowledging that the effort would be of no value.

As the tally of potential suspects slowly continued to inch upward, city papers introduced worried Clevelanders to a wide range of sexual deviants—some truly dangerous, others merely pathetic. Most of these troubled people don't seem to have been considered viable suspects by the police; Beverly Potts's disappearance, however, spawned an almost morbid fascination in the press with sexual deviancy. Authorities responded to reports of a buck-toothed man in his early thirties who lured an unidentified ten-year-old girl into a clump of bushes at Rockerfeller Park and induced her to take off her clothes so he could photograph her. (The child was not molested or physically harmed in any other way.) Responding to a tip that a West Sider living close to Halloran Park had been trying to entice a little girl into his room, police raided the twenty-five-year-old's apartment—where they found a cache of photographs and magazine clippings showing nude children, as well as a full set of newspaper clippings pertaining to the Potts case—and took the unidentified man into custody for "intense" questioning. Lorain County probation officer Arthur R. Moos reported to Cleveland authorities that a nineteen-year-old known sex offender from Amherst, Ohio (a village southwest of Cleveland), who made periodic trips to Cleveland for mental treatments, had been "wild-eyed" and "badly rattled" in the days since Beverly Potts disappeared. Police finally tracked down a forty-six-year-old machinist employed by the railroad who had called the Cleveland Police Central Station every night after August 25, assuring authorities that Beverly Potts was not dead. Another police report in the Potts files, dated August 29, 1951, records a tip from a woman named Margarita Geisman about a man who climbed on a bus at the Lorain Avenue–West 117 Street intersection every day at 3:30 P.M. As the bus rolled south on West 117, Ms. Geisman noted, to her disgust, that the man openly played with himself while eyeing young girls under the age of twelve. The brother of one of Anita Potts's coworkers had once been implicated in a molestation affair, and though the unidentified man had never been in trouble again, he now found himself caught up in the police dragnet. The coworker vented her anger at Anita over her brother's treatment. None of these disturbed individuals could be tied to the vanished youngster.

A MYSTERIOUS BUNDLE IN THE CUYAHOGA RIVER

Tuesday, September 4, started out as a normal day for thirty-three-old Henry Palmer, a warehouse worker at the William Edwards Company on West 9. That afternoon, sometime between 2:00 and 3:00, he was working on the third floor at the back of the building when his eyes strayed to the window and the Cuyahoga River just outside. He saw a bundle of some sort being carried along slowly by the river's sluggish current. It was fairly large, perhaps as much as five feet long, and seemed wrapped in cloth; something was sticking out from either end. As the mysterious object drifted by, it struck Palmer that the thing looked suspiciously like a wrapped human body with arms and legs protruding from the ends of the bundle. Mrs. Ada Skrovan, operator of a forty-two-foot cruiser called

Checking out the mysterious bundle in the Cuyahoga River on Tuesday, September 4, 1951. From left to right: head of the homicide unit David Kerr, Cuyahoga County coroner Samuel Gerber, and warehouse worker Henry Palmer, who first reported seeing the large, floating mass. *Cleveland Press* Archives, Cleveland State University.

the *Ada,* also watched as the strange-looking package floated by. It was wrapped in green canvas and tied with rope, she later told police.

With McArthur temporarily out of action due to exhaustion, Kerr headed up a team that raced to the Flats. Kerr questioned several onlookers and stationed men at the scene along the Cuyahoga where Palmer had first seen the strange object—in case it should reappear—as well as at various other boat landings along the river. Then, along with detective sergeant Theodore Carlson and men from the Coast Guard, Kerr cruised, and then finally dragged, the Cuyahoga in a fruitless search for the suspicious bundle. The next day, the men returned to the river but again found nothing. Whatever the mysterious package had been, it had apparently floated out of the river and disappeared in the vastness of Lake Erie. Although the press did not mention his presence, news photos show Cuyahoga County's long-serving coroner, Samuel Gerber, standing with the men of the search team.

BACK TO SQUARE ONE

Leads were drying up; clues were dwindling; viable suspects were few; intense questioning of witnesses and suspects had produced little solid information. Ten days from the time she had last been seen alive, the hunt for Beverly Potts ground to a halt. "Every day this thing gets more mystifying," McArthur complained to the *Press* on September 11. Authorities adopted the same strategy they invariably employed when investigations slowed to an impasse; they began retracing their steps, rechecking and reexamining everything to make sure no small detail, no fleeting hint had passed by them unnoticed. Police officers went door-to-door requestioning all the Potts neighbors. "The rechecking program is possibly the most detailed search ever undertaken by Cleveland police," commented the *Plain Dealer* on September 11. Authorities put as positive a spin as possible on this regrouping; on September 3, McArthur met with Mayor Burke and Safety Director Al Sutton (who had been minimally involved in the investigation up to this point) at City Hall—an official meeting well publicized by the city press. The chief of detectives had expressed his dismay that of the estimated fifteen hundred Showagon attendees at Halloran on the night of August 24, only about twenty-five people had come forward. (There was at least one reasonably well-documented instance of a young witness keeping a Beverly sighting to himself because his father did not want to get involved.) Mayor Burke, therefore, reached out to the public. "I am now appealing to every person who was there to call McArthur at Central Station and arrange a time for an interview. This appeal is made to everyone—whether he saw Beverly or thinks he has any information or not." (A few days before, McArthur had declined taking such a step. Now, on top of everything else that he was doing, McArthur seemed serious in his intention to guide personally an interview process potentially involving well over a thousand witnesses. If such was indeed the case, he was either extremely dedicated to solving the Beverly Potts mystery or very determined to protect his turf—perhaps, a bit of both.)

Safety Director Sutton assured anxious Clevelanders—who may have begun to question, however quietly, the effectiveness of their police force—that the intense efforts to find Beverly or her abductor would not be relaxed. When pressed by reporters, Mayor Burke acknowledged some serious thought had been given to carrying out a house-to-house search, but all involved had backed away from the idea—at least, for the time being. "That's a tough and touchy problem. But I have been considering it. I know that some police officers are against it. There are legal questions involved, it will be on a voluntary basis—that is, people will have to let us in their houses just to help us out."

But what seemed impossible, or at least questionable, on September 3 became a reality eleven days later; on September 14, police began what the press termed a basement-to-attic search of the homes on Linnet Avenue. Police officials justified the unorthodox action by pointing out that Beverly might have been coaxed into a neighbor's house by someone she knew, and by insisting that professional investigators could pick up on a clue that had escaped the untrained eye. Authorities also raised the admittedly flimsy possibility that the child might be hiding in the neighborhood during the day and slipping into neighborhood houses at night. "This is being done with the consent of the home owners," McArthur assured worried civil libertarians. "We can't go in if people refuse admission. But I'm assigning 10 of my most diplomatic detectives." A week before, on September 7, three unidentified "high-ranking police officers" (no doubt including McArthur) gave the Potts home another thorough going-over to make sure previous searches had not missed something potentially significant. "We checked the dust on the basement windows," McArthur commented to the *Plain Dealer* on September 8, "to make certain the child was not still in the neighborhood and possibly hiding in the home at night."

Outside on the street, reporters from the three Cleveland dailies grew bored and weary. They had quickly exhausted whatever flicker of tolerance they may have enjoyed initially in the Potts home by settling in and using the house as a base of operations with little regard for the feelings of the family. The city's hard-bitten newshounds tramped in and out of the tiny dwelling in shifts and, according to Anita, acted is if they owned the place. "I was very unhappy that they took such liberties in our house," she declares half a century later. "There were reporters sitting in the house waiting for the phone to ring with news. I thought it was horrendous. The reporters seemed to have no regard for our family. They were conducting business on their own." After about a week of unwelcome occupation, "We invited the reporters out," she reflects emphatically. For another week or so, they milled around on Linnet Avenue in front of the Potts home trying to drum up story angles and ferret out leads. Finally, some of the neighbors across the street (principally Ann Cossano, who lived almost directly opposite from 11304) allowed them to sit on their front porches. The voluminous front-page coverage of Beverly's disappearance during the first few days after August 24 had created a monster, and now the monster had to be fed. But information was hard to come by. There were no organized daily press briefings, and the police were not always cooperative. McArthur could usually be counted on to pass out some useful bits, but if he happened to be busy or in a bad mood, he wouldn't think twice about throwing a reporter out of his office or telling him to go to hell. It was also not easy to gain access to members of the Potts family, and most of the Linnet Avenue residents were not particularly inclined to talk to the press. Rumors ranging from plausible to ridiculous swirled through the neighborhood. In such a tight-lipped atmosphere, any nugget of information, any hint of a lead automatically assumed enormous value, but reporters had few options available for verifying the details. Doris O'Donnell Beaufait recalls that she and her colleagues began manifesting the giddy symptoms of gallows humor sometimes common in such tragedies. They manufactured all sorts of bizarre and improbable explanations for Beverly's disappearance and her current whereabouts. Ultimately, they concocted a wild tale that Robert Potts had dispatched his daughter and buried her in the basement. As a joke, they dressed up this crazy scenario as a lead they had stumbled upon and passed it on to the police officers on the scene. The story was apparently cooked up during the first week of September, for when McArthur and other police officers arrived to reexamine the Pottses' home on the seventh, the assembled reporters wrongly assumed—to their mingled horror, amusement, and embarrassment—that they had come to dig up the Potts cellar.

"IF WE COULD HAVE THE BODY OF OUR CHILD"

"We have finally come to the realization that we will never see our Beverly alive again." Cleveland radio stations carried this poignant plea from the Potts family on September 1, coincidentally the same day that *News* staff reporter Howard Beaufait wrote, "And I am certain of only one thing. Beverly Potts will not be returned to her home alive." It remains unclear from the press coverage, however, whether the Pottses' appeal was read by an announcer or made directly by a member of the Potts family. By mid-September, the circus on Linnet Avenue had died down. Cars no longer cruised the street; the morbidly curious no longer came to stand outside the Potts home and gawk. Police removed the barriers at both ends of the block. When the children returned to school on September 10, Louis Seltzer apparently decided there was little to be gained from paying a battalion of his reporters and photographers to hang around the street and sit on Ann Cossano's front porch, so he called them back to the *Press* offices. The staff writers from Cleveland's other two dailies also abandoned their two-week Linnet Avenue sit-in and returned to other stories. But the assembled writers carried away with them some curious, even dark personal impressions that never found their way into print. Although everyone in the neighborhood knew and liked Beverly, few, if any, seemed well acquainted with her parents. Robert Potts was regarded as virtually a stranger on Linnet Avenue, perhaps because of his erratic work schedule at the Allen Theater. The reporters saw him as gruff, grim, distant, and unwilling to communicate. "A typical beaten down housewife," grumbled one observer about Potts's wife, Elizabeth. When there are few if any facts with which to work, rumor and innuendo will rush to fill the void. All the members of the Potts household had been subjected to lie-detector tests by police, and when those initial interviews proved somehow inconclusive because of mechanical problems with the machine, each member of the Potts family was reexamined individually at an undisclosed eastside location. Anita Potts vividly remembers the squad car pulling up unannounced outside the office of the National Cash Register Company, her employer, to escort her to this mysterious spot. "I had gone back to work by then downtown. And this police car drives up on the sidewalk of Euclid Avenue, which is a huge thoroughfare in Cleveland, a main thoroughfare." News and half-truths about both the initial examinations and the retests undoubtedly filtered down to the residents of the Linnet Avenue neighborhood. According to police reports, there were dark murmurings about intense marital discord in the Potts family and even blacker suggestions that Robert Potts had a serious drinking problem that had resulted in multiple DUI arrests. (A police check of traffic violations revealed, however, that he had been cited only once, for making an improper left turn. And alcohol had not been a factor.) "There's something about the Pottses," confided one neighbor conspiratorially to reporters. Was there ever any justification for such musings, or does the statement remain a malicious bit of gossip—perhaps, someone's selfish, thoughtless attempt to ingratiate him or herself with the members of the press? It hardly seemed to matter. By then, for both press and public, the official view of the Potts family members had been carved in stone; they were sympathetic victims. But for the next fifty years, admittedly vague and fleeting suspicions about the Potts household would sometimes hover distantly around the Beverly Potts legend. Even as late as 2002, someone regarded me quizzically as I was pursuing my research and asked, "Wasn't there something about her father?"

NOTES

Howard Beaufait's piece on the Beverly Potts–Melvin Horst parallels appeared in the September 15, 1951, edition of the *News*.

The tale of the man with the pointed chin got a thorough going-over in all three Cleveland papers. Official documents indicate that two other boys, Carl Hunt (Robert's brother) and James Herkes, were questioned at the same time as Robert Hunt, Ronald Bruggman, Richard Lutian, and Joseph Arcuri. In fairness, I should also point out that the surviving police reports dealing with the incident manifest considerably less outrage over Robert Hunt's fabrication than the city's dailies, dismissing the whole story as simply the product of overactive imaginations.

The text of Mayor Burke's appeal appeared in the *Press* on September 3. Safety Director Alvin Sutton's position in the Beverly Potts investigation seems to have remained entirely ceremonial. He was an ex-FBI man whose primary interest continued to be organized crime. After Sutton's death in 2002, Rebecca McFarland, local historian, authority on Eliot Ness, and member of the board of trustees for the Cleveland Police Historical Society, had a chance to go through the ex-safety director's voluminous files. Her admittedly rather cursory survey turned up nothing related to the Potts case.

McArthur's justification for the house-to-house search was carried in the *Press* on September 14.

Doris O'Donnell Beaufait of the *News* was among the newspaper people who gathered on Linnet Avenue for more than two weeks after Beverly's disappearance, and—though she could not recall specifically who may have felt or said what—she remembers the unchecked, poisonous swirl of rumors and the negative impressions some reporters and neighbors developed about the Potts family.

Anita Potts's recollection of the police arriving at the National Cash Register offices is part of her November 2003 taped conversation with Mark Wade Stone of Storytellers Media Group.

Clues from the Lake

The weather on Tuesday, October 9, was fair and pleasant; highs were in the sixties. During the afternoon, thirty-three-year-old Berea resident Robert J. Barnes—a dispatcher for United Airlines—stood near the navigation-light tower about three hundred feet offshore and cast his fishing line into the water at the mouth of the Rocky River. Suddenly, the tip of his pole responded to slight pressure and bowed gently toward the lapping water: there was something on the hook, but it was no fish. There was no struggling, just some slight resistance. Barnes reeled in his line and pulled a small piece of reddish cloth from his hook. He laid his prize on a rock, smoothed it out to dry, and again flicked his line into the river. When he went home that evening, he left his "catch" on the rocks. But something bothered him about that little piece of waterlogged cloth. It was red. Beverly Potts had been wearing a reddish-pink jersey when she mysteriously vanished barely more than a month before; he remembered that later descriptions of her clothing mentioned that her underwear was red as well. Barnes immediately telephoned Cleveland police. All three Cleveland dailies covered the subsequent search.

Detective Lieutenant James K. Dodge sent a squad car to Barnes's Berea home to pick him up and return him to the spot where he had left the mysterious bit of red cloth. But it was gone: perhaps simply lost in the darkness, perhaps washed away by the waves. By 7:00 the next morning, James McArthur, David Kerr, and coroner Sam Gerber stood on the Erie shore and watched while men from the coast guard, under the command of William H. Bellow, boatswain's mate, dragged the bottom of the lake with three-pronged grappling hooks, hoping to snag Beverly Potts's remains. Bellow told the *Press*, "If her body is submerged here, it must be weighted down or wedged in a crevice between rocks and other debris." Slowly, methodically the giant hooks clawed their way across the bottom of the lake about five hundred feet from shore, occasionally catching and breaking on a submerged crevice or log. When coastguardsmen hauled in one of the wicked-looking hooks, they found an eight-by-four-inch piece of blue cloth (Beverly had been wearing a blue jacket and blue jeans the night she vanished.) A second hook surfaced with a putrid, waterlogged mass containing what looked like dirty human hair. "I'll need 48 hours to determine chemically whether the substance is flesh," the coroner told the *Press*. "But I am satisfied after the initial examination that we have found human hair." (Newspaper estimates ranged from twenty to one hundred strands.)

During the afternoon, the cold lake winds picked up, and waves crashed with greater violence against the five-hundred-foot stone pier at the mouth of the Rocky River. But McArthur, Kerr, and Gerber kept their silent vigil. Cars began to slow as they cruised by, and spectators began to gather on the beach. Quiet whispers floated through the crowd: "They're looking for Beverly Potts." Pleasure boats and canoes converged on the rim of the search area; planes dived from the sky for a closer look. When one of the grappling hooks apparently caught on something too heavy to pull to the surface, McArthur contacted Mayor Burke,

November 11, 1951. Diver Robert Baldrey descends into the murky waters of Lake Erie in search of Beverly's remains. *Cleveland Press* Archives, Cleveland State University.

who, in turn, made arrangements with the Merrit, Chapman, and Scott Corporation to send a diving crew to the search area. As night began to settle in, Robert Baldrey made three dives to the bottom of the lake over a two-hour period. Though the water was little more than ten-feet deep, it was cold and dark. Baldrey slowly lurched and crawled along the lake floor in his cumbersome diving gear, the murky silence broken only by the faint, hollow echo of his air bubbles rising to the surface. But he found nothing—not even the "heavy object" that had snagged the grappling hook earlier in the afternoon. The only rewards for his efforts were a leak in his suit and dark, endless expanses of rock and sand. In spite of weariness, frustration, and darkness, no one seemed willing to give up the melancholy search.

By the next day, however, all the promising bits of evidence had evaporated. The tantalizing piece of blue cloth had apparently come from a bathing suit. The strands of dirty hair turned out to be brown—not blond like Beverly's. The clump of material to which they were attached was not flesh—perhaps, nothing more glamorous than cardboard. Weary and disappointed, the searchers reluctantly abandoned their efforts. On October 11, the coroner told the *Plain Dealer*, "I have no reason now to believe a body was or is there."

The Crimes of Frank Dale Davis

In the predawn hours of Thursday, November 15, a lone Yellow Cab cruised south on West 117 Street, slowing slightly at the intersections so the driver could get a glimpse of the street signs. The taxi eventually turned left, and its headlights peered down the blackness of Linnet Avenue. An address is always difficult to find in the dark, but this morning there was no problem. The porch light at 11304 burned like a solitary beacon in a thick, black fog. At 5:00 A.M., the driver eased the cab up the driveway and waited. Almost immediately, a slightly hunched female figure in a brown dress, a black coat, and a white babushka walked slowly but determinedly out of the front door carrying a brown paper shopping bag obviously filled with something. A man helped the woman get into the backseat of the taxi. She leaned forward and quietly whispered an address to the driver. By 5:05 A.M., the cab was heading downtown on Lorain Avenue to 750 Prospect Avenue.

Between 5:00 and 5:15 A.M., detective sergeant Paul Robinson—holding a phone to his ear and armed with a rifle—kept his eye on Prospect Avenue from a vacant furniture store across the street from 750. A black man—dressed in a hunter's cap, jacket, khaki shirt, dungarees, and laced-up combat boots—walked nervously by the dark, empty window; as Robinson and three other detectives watched, the man paced by the storefront two more times. At 5:20, a Yellow Cab pulled up to the curb in front of the Finance Building on the opposite side of the street, and a stooped figure exited the vehicle carrying a shopping bag. Detective Robinson spoke softly into the receiver, broadcasting a "signal one" to Tom Story in the police radio room. Immediately, ten police cruisers and twenty-three armed detectives began to move carefully into position, encircling the entire area. By now, the mysterious black man had moved to the south side of Prospect and was standing at about 700. As the woman looked around her, he began slowly waving a white hand-kerchief back and forth around the level of his hips; the woman seemed not to notice. The black man crossed over to the north side of Prospect and stood in front of what was then known as the Taylor Arcade. He waved his handkerchief around in the direction of the woman more frantically; she hesitated but began walking in his direction. Suddenly, a bus and a CEI (Cleveland Electric Illuminating Company, the local power company) truck roared by, and the detectives stationed in the empty furniture store momentarily lost sight of the unfolding scene on the street. When the noisy distraction had passed, detectives saw the man walking toward a parking lot at East 6 Street with the woman fol-lowing dutifully behind. The climax of a torturous, weeklong drama was only seconds away.

Six days earlier, on Friday, November 9, Robert Potts was on the job at the Allen Theater when someone called him to the telephone at 4:00 P.M. or shortly thereafter. Why had the Pottses' home phone number been dis-connected, demanded the voice on the other end of the line? Robert responded quietly that the action had been in response to the sheer deluge of calls coming to the household in the days following Beverly's disappearance. If he ever wanted to see his daughter again, hissed the strange voice, Potts better have his phone reconnected by 3:30 P.M. the next day, raise twenty-five thousand dollars, and wait for instructions. "Don't tell the police or we'll cut the girl's throat," warned the mysteri-ous caller according to the *Press* on November 15.

If Robert Potts hesitated at all, it certainly was not for very long. He phoned James McArthur. The chief of detectives' eyes narrowed and his mouth tightened in grim fury as Potts relayed the harrowing details of the disturbing call. (Here, as elsewhere, I have taken the liberty to indi-cate what McArthur's reactions probably were. Doris O'Donnell Beaufait remembers him vividly and shared her impressions of him with me. The three Cleveland dailies also developed a fascination with the man leading the investigation and covered him in detail, often emphasizing his personality traits. A student of the Potts case comes away from the extended press coverage knowing McArthur very well, perhaps better than anyone else involved.) A few weeks before, perhaps as much as a month, Donald Sinclair, a Linnet Avenue resident and neighbor of the Potts family, had received a strikingly similar call during which he had been told to take the same set of instructions directly to Robert Potts. Sinclair did not contact Beverly's father, but he did report the incident to the police. The chances that any of this could actually lead to Beverly Potts's return ranged from exceedingly remote to nonexistent; McArthur immediately recognized that this was obviously a vicious hoax, an exceptionally cruel and crude extortion attempt. He was outraged. With typical zeal and dedication, McArthur immediately seized control of the entire matter. By the next day—Saturday—he got the telephone company to reconnect the Pottses' old number and dispatched detectives to both the Allen Theater and the Potts residence to monitor any incoming calls.

The next call came around 2:20 P.M. on Saturday, November 10, again to the Allen Theater. But Robert Potts was off somewhere in the recesses of the large building, and no one could find him. By the time a coworker had tracked him down, the line was dead. Police at the theater and the Potts home waited expectantly for hours, but the mysterious caller made no further attempts to contact Robert Potts that day. Sunday passed by, then Monday; still no further calls came from the unknown extortionist. Finally, on Tuesday, November 13, the phone rang at the Allen Theater around 10:40 A.M. A voice demanded to speak with Robert Potts. For the next half hour, Potts talked and argued with the man on the other end of the line. Twenty-five thousand dollars was impossible. There was simply no way Potts could raise that kind of money. The caller lowered his financial demands to ten thousand dollars and then offered to send the family a piece of the red "sweater" Beverly had been wearing on the night of August 24 to prove he, indeed, had the child. When Potts replied that his daughter had been wearing a red jersey when she disappeared, the man corrected himself and agreed that it was a jersey—not a sweater. He also offered to turn over a piece of Beverly's blue jacket. Then the conversation turned frightening and violent. The man asserted he had thirty-five men working for him, and if Potts so much as breathed a word of this to the police, especially to McArthur, they would cut Beverly's throat and deliver her to her family dead (a threat the caller was making for the second time), kidnap Robert's other daughter, Anita, and blow up the Potts residence. When Potts insisted he could raise no more than five thousand dollars, the mysterious caller questioned if he was really interested in seeing his daughter again. Before hanging up, the would-be extortionist informed Potts that he was acquainted with his wife, Elizabeth, and had just sent her a letter.

Detectives at the theater immediately drove to the Potts residence on Linnet Avenue and intercepted the afternoon mail. The envelope bore a postmark indicating that it had been mailed in Cleveland at 10:00 P.M. on Sunday. The strange piece of correspondence was neatly printed in pencil on a piece of ordinary writing paper. "Just to let you know your daughter Beverly is a very sick kid," began the deeply disturbing letter.

Your husband was called and told about it but refused to co-operate with us. He would rather play ball with the cops than us. We told him to connect his home phone and we would call him.

Now we want $25,000 cash in $5-$10 and $20 bills and don't try to hand us a stage Bankroll like they did in the Prell case last week [a reference to a recent extortion attempt involving a payoff with fake currency]. Because before we release Beverly we are going to count every dollar.

Just connect your phone up at home and don't let the cops tap the wire and play ball with us if you want your daughter back alive.

By the time the second call came in to the Allen Theater shortly after 5:15 P.M., the phone had been rigged so police could listen in on extensions. During the twenty-minute call, the extortionist seemed more disturbed than ever, criticizing the police and repeating his threat to bomb the Potts residence. The detectives listening to this diatribe thought there was something vaguely artificial about it, as if the caller were reading from something he had written out earlier. When Potts declared that he could not lay his hands on more than six thousand dollars, the man seemed to accept this reduction. "We will set up the situation for 5:30 A.M., Thursday, November 15. We know your wife and she knows us— although she will deny it," he stated. "The pickup will be made by a Negro man [who, the caller insisted, would know nothing of the affair because 'we could get any wine head to carry out our orders for a couple of bucks']. Have your wife standing in front of 750 Prospect Avenue at 5:30 A.M. She is to look in all directions, watching for a handkerchief. That is the signal." Three hours after the cash had been turned over to the unidentified "Negro man," Beverly would be released to her mother in front of the Terminal Tower. "We are not amateurs," insisted the caller. "We don't want you or your daughter to meet us. It has to be your wife." Then the seemingly disturbed man delivered a bizarre farewell

Bernhard Conely dressed as Beverly's mother Elizabeth for his part in the carefully planned sting operation that ultimately ensnared Frank Davis. *Cleveland Press* Archives, Cleveland State University.

before hanging up: "You will get no more word—this is the last. God bless you and you will have her three hours after we get the money."

By midnight, November 14, the police were in place in the vacant furniture store across from 750 and were carefully watching Prospect Avenue. A couple of hours before, a somewhat apprehensive detective Bernard J. Conley from the ballistics bureau had arrived at the Potts home. Inside the large bag he brought with him he had packed a brown dress, a pair of black shoes, and a black coat—all belonging to his mother—and a dummy package supposedly containing five thousand dollars in cash. He had never met nor even spoken to anyone in the Potts family, and he sat nervously watching the fights on TV with Robert Potts, while Elizabeth brewed coffee in the kitchen; he wondered if he should talk about the painful circumstances that had ultimately brought him to 11304 Linnet Avenue to impersonate Beverly Potts's mother. Conley sighed inwardly with relief when Robert Potts brought up the difficult subject himself. At 1:00 A.M., a weary Elizabeth Potts climbed the stairs to get a few hours of rest; her husband sat up with Detective Conley through the rest of the night.

At 4:00 A.M. Elizabeth called the Yellow Cab Company and asked that a taxi be sent to their Linnet Avenue address by 5:00; as she stood quietly in the kitchen brewing fresh coffee, Detective Conley began donning his mother's clothes over his tennis outfit and a sweat shirt. He strapped his service revolver under the heavy, black coat and then completed his disguise with a white babushka and a pair of his own glasses. He wobbled around a little until he got used to walking in the uncomfortable women's shoes. The cab arrived punctually at the appointed time. Elizabeth Potts smiled wanly at Conley as he prepared to leave the house. "You look pretty good," she said. It was no secret she wanted to take the dummy package of money to the drop spot herself, but there was absolutely no question that this was entirely a police matter. Shortly after 5:00 A.M., the taxi swung out of the drive and headed west on Linnet Avenue toward West 117 Street. Inside the quiet house, there was nothing for the Potts family to do but wait.

The drive downtown took less time than police had predicted, and the cab pulled to the curb at 750 Prospect at 5:18—more than ten minutes ahead of schedule. Apprehensive that his early arrival might somehow compromise the elaborately staged sting operation, Conley got out of the cab slowly and looked nervously around the dark street. Even with a sweatshirt and his tennis clothes under his disguise, he was cold; how do women stand this, he wondered. A solitary black figure stood several yards away, gently waving a handkerchief back and forth. But it was still too early, Conley thought, so he pretended not to notice the agreed upon signal. When the black man crossed to the north side of the street and began waving the handkerchief more vigorously, the detective felt he had no choice but to walk toward the solitary figure. Suddenly, a CEI truck and a bus thundered by, breaking the eerie early-morning silence; the black man again crossed Prospect and began heading toward a parking lot at East Sixth Street with Conley following behind at a discreet distance. Still watching from the darkness of the deserted furniture store, detective sergeant Paul Robinson could see Conley and their unidentified quarry walking through the East Sixth lot. He held the telephone receiver close to his mouth; "Signal Two," he whispered. Suddenly the black man picked up his pace, seeming to rush away from Conley. Perhaps he sensed that he had walked into a trap; but before he could react, detective Vincent Fiebig leaped from his squad car parked on Huron Avenue and leveled a shotgun at the would-be extortionist. Within seconds, several other police cars screeched to a halt and surrounded the empty parking lot. The first cop on the scene was the architect of this elaborate setup: McArthur stood before his flustered captive stone-faced, silent, and furious.

Shortly after noon, following seven hours of intense grilling by five detectives, Frank Dale Davis—a fifty-two-year-old ex-convict who lived with his wife, Mary Elisa, three stepchildren, and two grandchildren at 2530 East 33 Street—finally cracked. "I was strapped for money," he blurted later to the *Press*. "I wanted to get out of debt. I thought it would be a good way to pick up some money." Davis later told *Plain Dealer* reporter Nate Silverman and detective William Kaiser that he decided on this particular course of action because the story of the missing little girl was so "hot." (The mysterious telephone call to Donald Sinclair of Linnet Avenue demanding money had been his first attempt to put his plan in motion.) For seven hours, Davis had stubbornly asserted his innocence to the detectives, insisting that he knew nothing of the extortion calls to Robert Potts and happened to be on Prospect at that early hour of the morning because he was waiting for a ride to his job on a Miles Avenue project. Frank Davis sported the proverbial rap sheet as long as his arm. Stretching back to 1916, his record listed four juvenile and eleven adult arrests, resulting in stays in Ohio at the Hudson Boys Farm and Boys Industrial School in Lancaster as well as incarcerations at Mansfield for auto theft, the Ohio Penitentiary for housebreaking, and the Warrensville Workhouse for disorderly conduct, intoxication, vagrancy, and obtaining money under false pretenses. If all this were not impressive enough, there were also allegations of indecent exposure. At the time of his arrest for attempted blackmail of the Potts family, Davis worked as a laborer. When police searched his East 33 residence, they found a notebook whose paper matched the ransom letter.

Once Davis admitted his extortion attempt, reporters noted that he turned curiously, even remarkably, philosophical about his predicament. Mortgage and furniture payments ate up his entire sixty-five-dollar-a-week paycheck, he lamented, and he had fallen into debt. Davis planned to

James McArthur, architect of the elaborate sting operation, with his prize, Frank Dale Davis. *Cleveland Press* Archives, Cleveland State University.

explain his sudden riches to his creditors and friends by insisting he had hit the numbers. His bewildered wife, Mary Elisa, insisted she knew nothing of her husband's plot and had prepared his lunch for him that day as she always did. McArthur acknowledged that Davis knew nothing about the disappearance of Beverly Potts; he was nothing more than a brutally insensitive, and not terribly bright, opportunist. Police turned over all the facts in the entire episode to postal authorities and the FBI. Ironically, bail was set at twenty-five thousand dollars, the exact sum Davis had initially demanded from Robert Potts. At his arraignment on December 3, 1951, before Judge Edward Blythin, Frank Dale Davis pleaded guilty to a single charge of blackmail and extortion; eleven days later, he was sentenced to the Ohio State Penitentiary. He was paroled on July 1, 1957.

At the end of the day, Robert and Elizabeth Potts came to the central police station to make their official statements. Emotionally drained from the six-day ordeal, Elizabeth confided wearily to reporters, "All this time without any news is hard to bear. Each day brings a faint hope that someone will find her. But this attempt wasn't right. We don't have any money. I didn't have any hopes."

NOTES

Led by the *Press*, all three Cleveland Dailies devoted an enormous amount of space to the Davis plot. The *Press* even managed to talk Detective Conley into writing an article for the paper about his experience on November 11. As was invariably the case, the *Plain Dealer* exercised the most restraint in its coverage. Elizabeth Potts's final comments were carried in the *News* on November 15.

Frank Dale Davis's criminal record is on file in the Cuyahoga County Archives, Felony Record No. 61445.

Come Dressed as Beverly

On November 26, 1951, an anonymous man who identified himself only as "Tom from Youngstown" contacted Patsy Swing's father, Lester, by phone with a bizarre story and a sick request. His voice seemed muffled and distant—as if he were speaking through something being held over the mouthpiece of the phone. He had struck Beverly with his car on the night of August 24, he insisted; and in his panic, he had scooped up her seemingly lifeless body and taken it away. Beverly, however, had only been stunned; she eventually made a full recovery—except for the fact that she was now suffering from amnesia. The unidentified caller promised to return the confused child to her parents, but only if Swing was willing to follow his orders. He wanted Patsy Swing to dress up like Beverly on the night of her disappearance—the sole exception being that he requested a blue skirt in place of Beverly's blue jeans—and stand by the magazine counter at the May Company department store downtown Cleveland on Saturday, December 1, between 3:00 and 5:00 P.M. Once he saw Patsy in the specified costume, he would return with Beverly within ten minutes.

Swing immediately relayed the entire incident to Cleveland police. Authorities wanted to set up a sting operation only slightly less elaborate than the one that had netted Frank Dale Davis the month before and asked the worried father to allow his daughter to participate in the manner in which the mysterious caller had asked. Stoutly maintaining that they were unwilling to expose Patsy to any additional mental anguish or potential danger, Lester and Margaret Swing wisely refused. According to official records, authorities then asked the Swings for a recent photograph of Patsy so they could arrange for a convincing decoy. On the specified day, at the specified time, undercover cops watched intently as Margaret Kilbane from the Women's Bureau loitered in front of the May Company magazine counter dressed in the appropriate costume. Nothing happened. On December 12 Tom from Youngstown again contacted Lester Swing by phone and restated his demands; this time Patsy was to show up at the appointed spot at the time specified on Saturday, December 15. The Swings must have relented under heavy pressure from the authorities, for police reports indicate that Patsy did, indeed, dress in clothes resembling those Beverly had been wearing on the night of August 24—initially the pinkish-red turtleneck jersey was a problem since Patsy Swing did not own one—and assumed her position in the designated spot at the May Company. Detectives McNea, Savage, Anderson, and Moran—accompanied by several policewomen, including former decoy Margaret Kilbane—took up concealed positions around the magazine counter; Patsy's deeply concerned mother, Margaret Swing, hovered protectively nearby. Undoubtedly confused and frightened, Patsy Swing bravely stood her ground, though the anguish she surely felt from being dressed like her best friend on the fateful night of her disappearance must have been wrenching in the extreme. Unaware of what was going on, shoppers came and went throughout the afternoon absorbed in their own daily affairs; authorities watched for anything and anyone even remotely suspicious. When their attention gradually began to focus on a man lurking furtively around the scene, police swooped down and arrested forty-one-year-old Stephen Tyukody of Buckeye (a street on Cleveland's East Side) on the spot. The man had no previous police record; and though he admitted to placing the calls, he could provide no explanation for perpetrating his cruel scam. A subsequent lie-detector test absolved Tyukody of any involvement in Beverly Potts's disappearance.

Visions from the Spirit Realm

On September 25, 1952, an unidentified thirty-nine-year-old Parma house-wife and mother of two wandered slowly through the Metropolitan Park near Memphis Road in Brooklyn Village, on Cleveland's south side, in the company of her fifty-four-year-old husband. The woman kept search-ing the ground, looking at the trees, and scanning the horizon as if look-ing for something. The couple's seemingly aimless meandering ultimately attracted the attention of Brooklyn police sergeant Armond Hunnings. (Whether Hunnings happened to be in the park or had been called by someone else is not known.) When he approached the suspicious-look-ing duo and questioned them about their curious activity, he learned that the woman was a psychic. She had begun having psychic experi-ences in 1931 when she was nineteen years old, she said, and she and her husband—also a psychic—were in the park chasing a vision.

During the holiday season of 1951, the professed psychic explained, an attractive young girl wearing a white dress suddenly appeared in her home and watched shyly and silently as she decorated her Christmas tree. The girl wore her hair in long pigtails and was tall with large, wide-set eyes. She seemed sad. Without saying a word, the girl vanished as suddenly as she had appeared. Because of her intense interest in the case, the astonished tree trimmer immediately recognized the young girl as Beverly Potts, the missing child who had vanished three months before in August. Over the next few months, the specter had material-ized several additional times: gradually the psychic pieced together the child's grim story from a series of "spiritual conversations." Beverly, she insisted, had accepted a ride from an eighteen-year-old stranger in a green convertible, who—instead of taking her home as promised—had driven her to the park and killed her; but since her knowledge of earthly

September 27, 1952. A psychic's visions sent searchers digging in the Metro Parks for Beverly's remains. *Cleveland Press* Archives, Cleveland State University.

affairs ended with her death, the vision could not say where her body was buried. Finally, Beverly appeared holding a photograph showing a section of the park in Brooklyn Village, and now the psychic pair was searching for the spot that matched the spectral photo.

Today, most professional investigators would probably dismiss such a tale as the stuff of tabloids and daytime TV talk shows, but Sergeant Hunnings—a cop with an impressive arrest record built on following his hunches—took the whole thing seriously enough to follow the pair with a shovel as they ambled over the park terrain on their spiritual journey. Hunnings methodically dug into the earth whenever and wherever the psychics thought they recognized the area. As the trio wandered over the park ground, the woman's eyes suddenly widened in startled recognition; she had seen this particular drainage culvert in her vision. Nearby, the three searchers stumbled upon a partially burned leg from a pair of blue denim dungarees and a zipper. As night closed in, Hunnings summoned Brooklyn firemen to comb through the culvert. They poked, prodded, and dug around the entire area until gathering darkness rendered their efforts virtually impossible.

The next day, according to the *Plain Dealer*, Brooklyn Village safety director Joseph E. Murphy ordered a contingent of his policemen and firemen back to the park "on the remote possibility that the body may be there." The usually staid morning paper treated the excursion with bemused objectivity. "Several quite down-to-earth policemen and firemen of Brooklyn Village today will follow the 'visions' of a Parma housewife who maintains she has been in communication with the missing Beverly Potts." For the rest of the day, the army of searchers carefully explored the same ground covered by Hunnings and the psychic pair the night before. "A lot of water washes down Big Creek every spring," Murphy mused to the *Plain Dealer*. "It could be that the dungarees are hers and the body was lodged in a hollow or crevice which was searched earlier with no results." But the dungarees did not belong to Beverly Potts. Laboratory tests revealed the piece of denim had come from a pair of boy's jeans. At the end of the day, the search was called off. "We're grateful these visions were not seen on the city dump," quipped one veteran cop to the *Plain Dealer* on September 27.

The psychic Parma housewife and her husband were never publicly identified. Whether the pair simply retreated to their home in the West Side suburban neighborhood or kept searching on their own is not known. Nor was it ever reported whether or not Beverly continued her ghostly visits after the futile search was officially terminated. "I saw Beverly again last night," the woman reported to the *Press* on September 26 as the Brooklyn Village safety forces combed the park. "She was at the Potts home, crying, with her arms around her mother. But the mother didn't know, she isn't clairvoyant."

NOTES

All three Cleveland dailies devoted space to the hunt through the Brooklyn Village park (September 26–27, 1952). Interestingly enough, the *Plain Dealer's* coverage was the most detailed. Considering the level of the *Press's* rhetoric at the time of Beverly's disappearance, the paper's treatment of this particular episode of the tragedy was strangely muted.

"My name is Friday. I'm a cop!"

On August 20, 1953, local *Dragnet* fans, who regarded Jack Webb's dead-pan portrayal of Sergeant Joe Friday of Los Angeles's robbery and homicide unit as the last word in gritty cop realism, heard something unusual when the popular show concluded at 9:30 P.M. As the credits rolled, accompanied by the now-familiar, pounding *Dragnet* theme, a disembodied voice announced, "The police will give protection to a boy who calls himself Mr. X if he tells the truth." The impetus for this cryptic message had arrived at the *Press* offices the day before, on August 19. In a letter simply signed "Mr. X," an anonymous sixteen-year-old alleged that he had information for the police about the disappearance of Beverly Potts, but, fearing for his safety, he would only divulge it if authorities promised him protection. If the police agreed to his terms, they were to signal their acceptance by having this brief message read on the air at the end of NBC's *Dragnet* the following evening. WNBK station manager Jacob Hines agreed to this cloak-and-dagger request from Cleveland police, and the specified message went out over local air waves at the show's conclusion. Authorities waited, but no one came forward. Somewhere in the city, a cruel prankster probably reveled in his success. Two years after Beverly Potts's disappearance, official interest in her fate was still so strong that police readily snapped at his proffered carrot.

NOTES

The only documentation of this bizarre incident is a single police report from August 1953.

The Ballad of Harvey Lee Rush

Hard living and drinking had taken their toll on Harvey Lee Rush. Gaunt and white-haired, the transient looked twenty years older than his forty-some years. His wife had been killed in an accident; he had three teen-age daughters who he thought resided in Wilkes Barre, Pennsylvania, but he wasn't sure. Rush had drifted to Los Angeles in March 1955 after more than three years of aimless wandering around the country, princi-pally in the southeast. He supported himself in Los Angeles, more or less, by working as a hospital attendant. After a legion of run-ins with local police for intoxication over a nine-month period, authorities be-came fed up with him and ordered him out of the city. But Rush didn't have the money to go anywhere. The penniless vagrant unsuccessfully lobbied an ex-girlfriend in Cleveland for cash, coaxed twenty-five dol-lars out of his mother, then living in Bristol, Connecticut, and approached a Los Angeles mission center for additional travel funds. After center personnel told him to come back the next day, Rush met up with some drinking buddies and spent the little bit of money he had received from his mother on booze. Now staggering drunk, Rush blundered around a skid-row section of Los Angeles near Fifth and Crocker, where police picked him up in the early morning hours of December 11 and hauled him in for intoxication. Once at the station, however, Rush began mum-bling incoherently about having murdered a little girl in Cleveland.

Slowly, deliberately, the details of what Rush referred to as "my mur-der" began to emerge through a drunken fog. In July 1952 he had met a twelve-year-old girl during a puppet act at a "circus" who sported shoul-der-length brown hair and glasses, lured her away with candy, killed her, and buried her body under the "Rocky River Bridge at West 117th and Madison." With a three-page "confession" in hand, Los Angeles police contacted their Cleveland counterparts. Could this down-and-out drifter hold the key to the unsolved four-year-old mystery of Beverly Potts? Cleveland police were dubious; Rush's tale was hobbled by too many discrepancies. Beverly Potts was ten, not twelve; she had disappeared in August 1951, not July 1952; she had vanished from a Showagon performance, not a circus; there had been no puppet act (the *News* says there had been one); Beverly's hair was blond and cut short, not brown and shoulder-length; she never wore glasses; and there was no such bridge at the spot where Rush insisted on placing one. He could not give the girl's name nor even offer much of a description of what she looked like. He also varied his account of the clothes the girl was wearing from a skirt to overalls. As he sobered up, Rush gradually added more detail to his grim tale of kidnapping and murder. He had lured the unnamed girl away from the circus with a combination of ice cream and candy bars, induced her to walk with him to the Madison Avenue streetcar, and talked her into riding with him to the Rocky River Valley. Once there, they had waded across the river and settled down under a bridge in an area known locally as Sharkey's Hill. When the girl began to cry, Rush panicked and punched her in the head, apparently knocking her back against a rock. Fearing the girl dead, Rush quickly dug a shallow grave with his bare hands in the soft earth and buried her. The brutal crime, however, preyed on his mind, so he attempted to turn himself in to Cleveland police, specifically Officer "McCarthy." But police turned him away and told him to come back the next day. Rush lost his nerve, fled to New Orleans (where he said he tried to commit suicide), and ultimately wound up in Los Angeles. James McArthur and the rest of the Cleveland Police Department were dumbfounded. Was Rush simply a liar trying to perpetrate a hoax for some crazy personal reason (what sane person would confess to a killing?), or was he really a violent criminal who had committed a brutal murder in an alcoholic fog and was now trying to recall the four-year-old details through an equally dense and debilitating haze? There were just enough tantalizing details sprinkled in Rush's confused account to keep Cleveland authorities on the hook and from dismissing him and his story outright. He had given the girl's age as twelve. Beverly was ten but tall for her age; she could easily be mistaken for twelve.

A check into Rush's background revealed a personal local history as colorful and sordid as his life in Los Angeles. Also known as Henry Rushkowski, Harvey Rice, and Henry Ruzowski, Rush was born in Hartford, Connecticut, on December 17, 1907; he had drifted to Cleveland in 1930, where he piled up an impressive police record: an arrest for armed robbery in 1930 and no fewer than 104 incarcerations—including three stays in the workhouse—for intoxication since 1941. During his years in Cleveland, Rush called a dozen different addresses home, some of them frighteningly close to the Potts residence on Linnet Avenue. He had been examined by the County Psychiatric Clinic in 1953 for alcoholism and had spent time in Sunny Acres Hospital where he was diagnosed as tubercular. Over the years, several area hospitals had employed him as an attendant. From March 1950 to April 1951, Rush worked as a curtain hanger at the Hotel Cleveland. He had failed to show up for work one day and hadn't been seen since.

Ever the cautious professional, McArthur told the *Press* on December 12, "I'm not going off the deep end about this thing until I have the man's statement before me and something more tangible to go on." The savvy chief of detectives hedged his bet. While he blasted holes in Rush's story, he sent Detective George Gackowski to Los Angeles to check out Rush and his story in person and dispatched a search team to photograph the Rocky River Valley floor. (McArthur sent the photos and a detailed map of the area to Gackowski in Los Angeles to see if Rush could pinpoint the location where the alleged incident occurred. At least for the time being, he declined to actually search for a grave.) Meanwhile, Los Angeles authorities hooked up the now sober but still shaky Rush to a lie detector and subjected him to an intense four-hour grilling. Three polygraph experts, described as among the best in the country, administered the test and verified the startling results: Rush was telling the truth—or at least he thought he was. Sergeant Lee Scarborough of the Los Angeles Homicide Bureau told the *Plain Dealer* on December 12 that "as far as the machine is concerned, he killed the girl." Lieutenant Arthur G. Hertel confirmed to the *Press* the same day, "The man believes his story. He's either living a dream or telling the truth." Polygraph expert Frank Ireland agreed, "The machine would say Rush is truthful," but hedged, "but I'm not saying that." No one in either city had any idea how much Rush may have read about Beverly Potts's disappearance, and no one could be sure how deluded he might be. Given his mental state and still shaky condition, Los Angeles authorities decided to retest Rush later in the day.

"I'm not convinced either way," Gackowski reported back to McArthur by phone on December 15, according to the *Press*. "One minute you

Twilight of Innocence

believe him and then next minute you feel like walking away." Such inconclusive opinions left McArthur between the proverbial rock and a hard place. On December 15, police chief Frank Story told the *Press* that unless Gackowski could crack Rush's story completely "we will have to bring him back to clear away all doubts." Both McArthur and David Kerr concurred: "I think his story is 90% bull," McArthur raged to *Plain Dealer* reporter Pat Garling on December 16. "I think he is a pathological liar who is having trouble remembering the first lies he told in his original story," he fumed. "But," he added with a deep sigh of resignation, "we owe it to Beverly Potts' parents and I owe it to myself to bring him back here. That's the only way we can be 100% certain." Kerr agreed. "I believe there's only one way of settling this for everyone's peace of mind," he told the *News* on December 15. So it was decided. Los Angeles authorities would drop the intoxication charges; Rush would not fight extradition; and Detective Gackowski would bring the suspected murderer back to Cleveland for further examination.

There is a curious footnote to the entire Rush episode. On December 13 Kerr told the *Plain Dealer* that he wasn't interested in Rush and his confession because, in the Potts case, "no homicide has yet been shown." Such, indeed, is standard Homicide Bureau practice: no body, no involvement! But "standard procedure" hadn't stopped Kerr from becoming deeply immersed in the Potts investigation approximately a week after the child's disappearance on August 24, 1951. And there was no proof then, either, that a murder had been committed. By the time Rush was flown to Cleveland on December 15, however, Kerr's interest had obviously been rekindled. He was at the airport with McArthur to meet the flight from Los Angeles. (Had he simply had second thoughts, or did someone with a lot of political clout—Louis Seltzer or police chief Frank Story, George Matowitz's successor—take the chief of homicide to the woodshed sometime between December 13 and 15?)

The moment Rush stepped off the plane, he dropped a bombshell. His whole story had been a lie, he admitted. Having read just enough about the Potts case to fake a confession, he made the whole thing up in a sleazy attempt to get a free trip back to Cleveland for the holidays. Rush assumed that, once back in the city, he could recant his story and go free. His biggest concern was that police would beat him up once they learned of his deception. "I nearly went through the roof of the car," McArthur raged to the *Press* on December 16. "Kerr yelled at him." But he assured the press that no one would lay a hand on Rush—no

Con-man Harvey Lee Rush (left) arrives at Cleveland Hopkins Airport from California, accompanied by James McArthur (right) on December 17, 1955. Judging from the smile on McArthur's face, Rush had not yet dropped his bombshell. *Cleveland Press* Archives, Cleveland State University.

matter how angry they were. POTTS HOAX HEEL COOLS HIS IN JAIL AS POLICE DEBATE, read the headline of a December 17 *Plain Dealer* story. But there didn't seem to be much that authorities could do. "There's nothing we can do to Rush legally," Chief Story lamented to the *Press* on December 16. "His false police report was made in Los Angeles—not here." McArthur was furious. "It was a horribly cruel thing he did, bringing all this torture back to the minds of the parents of Beverly Potts at Christmas time," he complained to the *Press* on the same day.

There was no way the still grieving Potts family could have avoided knowledge of Harvey Lee Rush and his confession. The whole affair had been splattered over the front pages of all three Cleveland dailies beginning on December 12. Even before the lurid tale had been made public, the *News* took upon itself the duty of breaking the story to the Potts household. The passage of four years had not lessened the pain that hung over the small house at 11304 Linnet Avenue. Elizabeth Potts broke into sobs when informed of the alcoholic drifter's admissions. "Her father and I have never given up hope that some day the murderer will be found," she confided to the *News* on December 12. "We do still have hope." Two days later, *Press* reporter Robert Modic reluctantly returned to the West Side neighborhood. On August 24, 1951, he had watched Elizabeth Potts stand on her front porch wringing her hands as her eyes desperately searched the stretch of Linnet Avenue that led west to Halloran Park. Now, more than four years later, he stood on the same front porch. Looking haggard and far older than her fifty-five years, Beverly's mother regarded the reporter with a sad and vacant stare. "I don't think this man did it," she mumbled. "That story about luring her with candy—Beverly never would do that." Then, almost as an afterthought, she added softly, "We have to go on living." Elizabeth Potts died five months later in May 1956.

NOTES

All three Cleveland dailies devoted a great deal of space to the Harvey Lee Rush affair, December 12–17, 1955. There are also a number of reports in the Beverly Potts files that demonstrate how thoroughly Cleveland police looked into Rush's background. As is the case with other major pieces of the investigation, however, those reports are not kept together but dispersed among several different files. The case records also contain a series of unidentified photographs, possibly copies or the photos of the Rocky River Valley floor that James McArthur ordered taken and sent to Los Angeles.

From the Burlesque Stage
to the Grease Pit

Alleged Beverly sightings and bizarre explanations for her still-undetermined fate continued to proliferate for years. In spite of the dry formality of the language in the surviving police reports, many of the recorded tips make fascinating reading, even though none of them ever led to a break in the case. A Cleveland couple vacationing in Buffalo, New York, attended a burlesque review at a local theater in June 1952 and thought they recognized Beverly among the dancers. In August of the following year, an unidentified man informed Cleveland authorities that Beverly had been killed and stuffed into a furnace by an old man whose son happened to be a policeman. Hence, a cover-up. He had come upon this bit of intelligence while he and his daughter were questioning a Ouija board. In the same month, a woman named Ellen West wrote police that she had dreamed Beverly was buried in the Metro Parks. In 1955 the new owners of an old house on Scranton Avenue alerted police when they found an impressively large cache of newspaper clippings dealing with the Beverly Potts case, as well as a pink T-shirt, a pair of jeans, and some white tennis shoes under the floorboards in the bedroom. The couple became even more alarmed when the house's previous owner reacted strongly to their renovation plans that included digging up the basement to make it larger. "Don't do it," he emphatically ordered. The lead apparently went nowhere. March 2, 1956, brought a tip about a mysterious Edward Jones, a man sporting a record of arrests for rape, "sodemy [sic]," burglary, and shoplifting. An official check of the Potts files in 1956 revealed that his name had come up twice during the original investigation in 1951, but—inexplicably—the suspect had never been apprehended and questioned. In November 1958, Cleveland police turned their attention to a thirty-seven-year-old Chagrin Falls resident, then on parole for raping his daughter, because his ex-wife had falsely accused him of murdering Beverly and burying her body on a Chardon farm.

The leads continued to trickle in into the 1960s. In July 1960, Velma Turney of West 118 Street informed police that she had returned from church one Sunday morning almost a decade before only to be confronted by the unmistakable, sickening stench of burning human flesh. Deeply worried and not a little curious, the woman crept silently into her basement and caught her husband standing grimly by the furnace. Mrs. Turney went on to assure the authorities that, upon further reflection, she realized her suspicious husband always found a reason to leave the city every time there was a new upsurge of publicity about Beverly Potts's disappearance. On July 11, 1960, a New Jersey woman wrote Cleveland police to implicate her husband, Jerome, in the nine-year-old Beverly Potts mystery. Over the years, he had been arrested on a number of occasions for "lewdness" and "indecent exposure" to young girls—the first time in Cleveland, in Lakewood's Andrews Park on September 15, 1951, just three weeks after Beverly's disappearance. The writer maintained she had been harboring suspicions about him in the Potts case for some time. Detective Sergeant Norman Ferris and detective James Heppl traveled to Oradell, New Jersey, to check out the vaguely tantalizing tip. They questioned family members, mental health professionals who had treated the suspect, and finally the suspect himself; but they could not connect the man—though he was now confined to a New Jersey mental hospital and apparently was, indeed, a pervert—to Beverly's disappearance. In April 1962 Inspector Richard Wagner, head of the detective bureau, dispatched Detectives Thomas Coughlin and Edward O'Malley to Medina, Ohio, a town just south of Cleveland, because of a telephone tip that alleged Beverly Potts was alive and well and living there. Medina residents John and Pearl Potts had to produce papers to prove that their nineteen-year-old daughter Beverly Ann (rather than Beverly Rose) Potts was not Cleveland's most famous missing child. Cleveland police received an FBI form letter on February 3, 1961, alerting them that older missing-person notices in the bureau's Identification Division were being discarded or updated. Did local authorities want the bureau to keep the file on Beverly Potts open? In December 1962, police were assured that Beverly could be found buried under Musicarnival, an East Side summer performance venue on Warrensville Road. In August 1973 Pittsburgh police informed Cleveland authorities that they had a fifty-some-year-old bricklayer in custody who was complaining loudly

that police were following him because of what he knew about the
Beverly Potts case. Thorough questioning by Pittsburgh authorities produced a tale of kidnapping, murder, and dismemberment so confused
and rambling that it wasn't even clear whether the bricklayer was claiming to have been an active participant or merely an onlooker. His knowledge of the Potts case, however, proved sufficiently extensive to warrant
further interrogation by Cleveland police. But after traveling to Pittsburgh to question the suspicious character, Detectives Joseph Laub and
Louis Gancia decided the man was "a mental case," perhaps even suffering from a "split personality."

In mid-April of the same year, an unidentified Chardon woman, who
insisted she had known Beverly as a child, wrote Cleveland police informing them that she believed the missing girl had been murdered
and her body buried in a "grease pit," now a part of Jim's Custom Body
Shop on West 52 Street. The venerable structure to which the anonymous writer sent authorities stood at 1966 West 52 Street and had been
a blacksmith shop in horse and buggy days. The building had later been
converted to a service station, and, according to the press, in 1973 its
owner had retired to Arizona but had operated the garage up until shortly
before Beverly's disappearance in 1951. Jim Sledz, who in 1973 was rent-
ing the building, informed police that the grease pit had still been there
when he took over the space, so he filled it in—though with what he
apparently did not say—and covered it with boards.

On April 18 Lieutenants Ralph Joyce and Stanley Deka, as well as
Detectives Eugene Terpay and Ralph Armstrong, headed out to West 52
Street armed with the necessary picks and shovels to check out the
Chardon woman's tip. They started the dirty, backbreaking excavation
around 9:00 A.M. After digging down five feet, they struck the pit's original concrete floor; once past that imposing obstacle, they dug out another three feet before giving up the frustrating search. "We are satisfied
we have exhausted any possibilities raised by this clue," a weary Lieutenant Deka told the *Press.*

Another story circulating in the Cleveland police underground would
at first glance seem an entirely different incident, but there are enough
similarities of time, place, and detail to suggest that this tale is merely a
bowdlerized oral version of the grease-pit investigation as outlined in
the press and official reports. According to this "shadow version," in
the early 1970s there was a gas station on Lorain Avenue (1966 West 52
is just north of Lorain) whose proprietor supplemented his income by

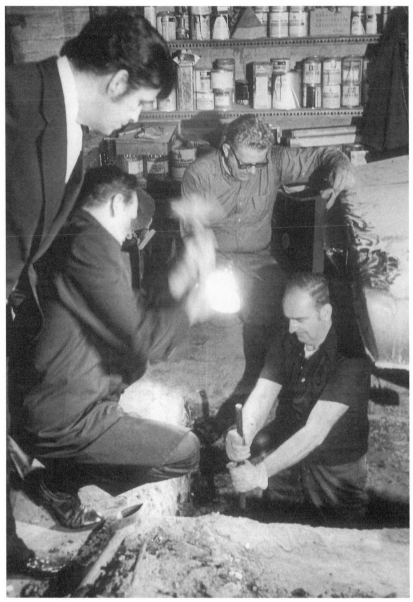

April 20, 1973. A tip led police to an old grease pit, once part of a service station, on West 52 Street just off Lorain Avenue. Ironically, Elizabeth Potts's family, the Treuers, had occupied the adjacent dwelling from the early 1920s. From left to right: Ralph Joyce, Stanley Deka, Eugene Terpay, and Ralph Armstrong. *Cleveland Press* Archives, Cleveland State University.

buying old American luxury cars, reconditioning them, and selling them to communist Eastern European governments, apparently to use as taxicabs or, perhaps, official limos. Though not illegal, one did have to possess a license to practice this trade—something the operator of the Lorain gas station had conveniently ignored. As long as he kept his nose clean, authorities apparently looked the other way; but once having run afoul of the law over some minor infraction, police moved quickly to close down his limo business and—adding insult to injury—informed the hapless proprietor he would have to dig up his old, leaky gas tanks and replace them with newer fiberglass models, an undertaking that would cost several thousand dollars. Not having the funds to comply, the gas station owner bided his time and then anonymously phoned city police with a tip that Beverly Potts's body was buried on the property. Thus police arrived and dug up the offending gas tanks for him at city expense.

There is a curious footnote to this entire incident that the press reports of the day did not pick up. The 1966 West 52 Street address is where Martin Treuer, Elizabeth Potts's father, settled his family after moving to Cleveland in the early 1920s. (Actually, the building had been purchased originally by Joseph Treuer—Martin's son and Elizabeth Potts's brother—and his wife, Rose. The elder Treuer and his wife seemed to have moved in about the same time, as did Elizabeth and her sister, Katherine. In 1973 Joseph Treuer, now living in Arizona, still owned the building—a fact the press missed—and was, therefore, the landlord who rented the space to Jim Sledz sometime after 1951.) The one-time blacksmith shop and service station also housed two apartments—one upstairs, the other downstairs. In 1951 Beverly's cousin Amber Lathan—the same Amber Lathan with whom she had gone to Halloran Park on August 23, the day before she vanished—and her family occupied the downstairs suite. Beverly, in fact, had been a frequent visitor. In 1973 Amber Lathan—now Amber Ware—was still living in the upstairs apartment, a circumstance that the *Press* duly noted. Who was the unidentified woman from Chardon, the original source of the tip? And why would she connect Beverly's disappearance to a building that, by 1973, had been in the Treuer family for fifty years?

NOTES

The vast majority of the information detailed in this chapter is drawn from the relevant police reports in the Beverly Potts case files. A *Plain Dealer* article by Pat Garling dated July 9, 1960, provides additional details concerning the suspect identified as Jerome, then housed in a New Jersey mental hospital; and an unsigned piece in the April 18, 1973, edition of the *Press* covers the excavation of the grease pit at 1966 West 52nd. The tale of the gas tanks was given to me by a Cleveland police officer who wished to remain anonymous. Anita Potts provided the history of her family's residency at the 52 Street address beginning in the early 1920s.

Notes from Hell

During Jack the Ripper's brief reign of terror in London's East End at the close of the nineteenth century, George Lusk, head of the Whitechapel Vigilance Committee received a letter whose salutation read, "From Hell Mr. Lusk." The sloppily written note is among the most famous of the Ripper letters, but whether it actually came from the hands of the infamous slasher has always been a point of debate among Ripperologists. But the taunting reference to Hell, with all its attendant associations of pain and suffering, caught the public fancy; and eventually police and public alike began to think of all the various pieces of Ripper correspondence as having come "From Hell." Beginning in the 1950s, bizarre notes connected to the Potts case began popping up virtually everywhere. The various texts of these hoaxes range from the merely stupid to the heartlessly cruel, and all of them have been dutifully filed away by Cleveland police officers among the Beverly Potts case records.

On May 3, 1952, twelve-year-old Eric Taylor and ten-year-old Billy Wargo stood on the Erie shore pelting an instant-coffee jar with stones. When the two boys finally retrieved their target, they found it contained a note. "To whom it may concern;" it read. "I am being held prisoner at a [sic] old boathouse about two mi. west of Cleveland." Dated August 28, 1951, the curious note was signed "Beverly Potts." Handwriting expert Clarence Hayes compared the penmanship of the note to samples of Beverly's writing and then informed McArthur that, though he detected similarities between the note and specimens that definitely came from the missing girl's hand, there were not enough of them for him to say with certainty that Beverly Potts actually wrote it.

On March 26, 1953, a customer found a note in a Willoughby, Ohio (east of Cleveland), gas station that read "To Whom It May Concern; I

Ray Biggio would like to confess to the murder of Beverly Potts hows [sic] body will be found in the dump on St. Clair Ave." (The "St. Clair Ave." to which the writer referred was in Willoughby, not Cleveland.) While Willoughby authorities searched unsuccessfully through the designated dump, Cleveland police rummaged through the Potts files but could find no references to anyone named Ray Biggio. Remarkably, authorities eventually managed to trace the note to an eleven-year-old girl, a student at Immaculate Conception School. Surviving police records provide no explanation for the child's sick prank. One day later, on March 27, postal workers in Sandusky came across a message that had been written on a post-office blotter. "I do hereby confess to the slaying of that young girl," it began. "God and my conscience demand. So to whomever may read this do your damndest." Signed James Rutmeyer, the note sparked another fruitless investigation on the part of Cleveland police.

Strange notes continued to turn up through the mid-1950s into the early 1960s. On January 8, 1954, Detective Raymond Wohl went to Cleveland's Regent Hotel to check out a claim in a note the police had received that Beverly Potts was living there. On May 21, 1955, a patron in the Eastman Branch of the Cleveland Public Library at West 115 Street and Lorain Avenue uncovered a note tucked away in a book titled *The Fishing Cat*. "To who eva [sic] this may concern–please help me. I'm at E. 9 St. Cleve Beverly Potts." Police checked the handwriting against known samples of Beverly's penmanship and the signatures of those who had checked out the book, but nothing materialized. In late July 1957 Cleveland businessman Ralf Dunker checked into a Dayton hotel and found a note written on a Western Union form. "To Whom It May Concern," ran the opening. "I killed and murdered Miss Beverly Potts Cleveland Ohio." The author of this brief confession had signed it simply, "Guess Who." On July 18, 1960, Robert Potts received an exceptionally cruel, anonymous letter informing him that Beverly had been picked up by a man in jeep and driven to a garage at West 115th and Lorain Avenue, where she was ultimately abused, murdered, and buried. By 1960 Robert Potts had been living alone in the small Linnet Avenue house for five years. His younger daughter had vanished without trace in 1951; his surviving older daughter had left Cleveland in 1952 because of her job; his wife had died, quite literally of grief, in 1956. The long-suffering father turned the sick note over to police, but nothing ever came of it.

The most recent "note from hell"—actually a voluminous letter of thirty-two hand-printed pages—appeared in the homicide unit of the

Cleveland Police department in July 2002. In this imposingly massive document, the writer spins out a tale of such grisly horror that it would cause even devotees of the most gruesome slasher films to wince in disgust. The author attributes Beverly's death to a one-time, reclusive West Sider who practiced witchcraft, buried body parts in his garage, and "has killed 18 people, men, women and children of all ages." The writer shifts the events at Halloran Park to Cleveland Heights on the city's East Side and mingles the details of Beverly's disappearance with the 1948 murder of Shelia Ann Tuley. Clearly, however, this was not intended as a hoax. The writer identifies herself by name and provides police with both her address and telephone number, all of which check out. The woman obviously believes the story she has shared with authorities fervently, and one can only wonder what inner demons or distorted, painful memories triggered an outpouring of such unrelenting horror.

The records of all these notes and letters, as well as the subsequent investigations into them, are part of the Beverly Potts case files.

PART THREE

The Persistence
of Memory

1974

The Maple Heights Molester

A concerned Cleveland lawyer contacted the police sometime in 1974. He was worried about a letter he had just received from the brother of a former client, a man he had apparently once represented in a child abduction and molestation case. The man in question had fled Cleveland in 1966 after being indicted in the abduction of two girls, their names and ages unknown. (The only sources for this chapter in the Beverly Potts saga remain local newspaper reports written six years later, in 1980. Everything about the story remains extremely sketchy. Neither the lawyer, nor the letter writer, nor the former client is identified. It isn't even clear exactly when in 1966 the charged "client" fled the city, but the skimpy details suggest he bolted after indictment but before trial.) In his missive to his brother's one-time legal counsel, the writer details his sibling's travels once he left Cleveland. Initially he settled in Detroit, where he changed his name, altered his appearance with a wig, and became a real estate agent. He later went to Tennessee, though what prompted the move or what he did once he got there is never explained. Sometime during this secret odyssey, the man married and fathered two daughters. In 1974 he decided to return to Cleveland, specifically Maple Heights, a suburb on the city's East Side. Before departing Tennessee, however, he told his brother (it is not at all clear where the man's brother was living) that he had kidnapped a little girl years before in Halloran Park. Lieutenant Edward P. Kovacic, head of the homicide unit, immediately assigned Detectives James M. Fuerst and Robert Shankland to track down and question the elusive suspect about the twenty-three-year-old, still-unsolved disappearance of Beverly Potts.

For three months, the pair of investigators dug into the man's background, unearthing a record of child molestation that included a stint in the Ohio Penitentiary about the time Beverly vanished in 1951. Finally, one evening Fuerst and Shankland went to the man's Maple Heights home and waited in his garage for him to return from work. As the suspect got out of his car, the pair of detectives approached and showed him their badges. What followed was incredible. According to the *Plain Dealer*, the man seemed almost relieved. "You finally got me. I'm glad it's all over," he muttered. "We're here to talk to you about the disappearance of Beverly Potts," replied Detective Fuerst. "Was that her name?" the man asked with a sigh of resignation. Over the next couple of days, Fuerst and Shankland interrogated him, repeatedly questioning him about his possible involvement in the tragic events on the night of August 24, 1951. In the early 1950s the suspect had, he claimed, lived across the street from Halloran Park, where he regularly prowled in search of little girls he could lure to his car and molest. Once his demons were satiated, however, his better angels tormented him to such a degree that he considered "blowing his brains out."

The two cops were sure they had finally got their man. "Detective Fuerst and I discussed it many times after talking with him, and both of us were convinced that he was the man. He said he had memories of a girl named Beverly. He told us things about the crime which only someone who had been there would have known," Shankland insisted to the *Press*. Fuerst told the *Plain Dealer*, "He said he had flashes about a girl named Beverly. He didn't know her last name. When we asked whether he kidnapped her, he said, 'I might have . . . I don't remember.'" The make, model, and year of the car the man owned in 1951 even dovetailed with the infamous descriptions of the various automobiles seen lurking around Halloran Park the night Beverly disappeared. But the detectives could not build a plausible case against him, certainly not one they could take to court. Witnesses had either died or dispersed; the intervening decades had simply wiped away too much potential evidence. The man even offered to take a lie-detector test, but polygraph experts insisted that the passage of so much time would invalidate the results. Still, Fuerst and Shankland turned over what information they had to the county prosecutor's office. But, citing lack of evidence, assistant prosecutor Joseph Donahue ruled out taking the case to court.

All of this happened in 1974, but six years would pass before the story ever reached the public. On June 13, 1980, eight-year-old Tiffany Papesh disappeared from her Maple Heights home; and sometime during the ensuing flurry of media coverage of the investigation, the six-year-old story of the Maple Heights suspect in the Beverly Potts case broke in the press. Both the *Plain Dealer* and the *Press* scurried to interview Fuerst (then retired) and Shankland. BEVERLY POTTS' KILLER FOUND, FREED, POLICE SAY, roared the *Plain Dealer* on August 17, 1980; "Beverly Potts case believed solved, trial ruled out," responded the *Press* the following afternoon. Of course, the whole matter proved far more complicated than either headline suggested. Neither the Maple Heights police nor, apparently, the FBI were aware of the 1974 investigation; as far as Fuerst and Shankland knew, the unidentified suspect—now in his fifties—still lived in Maple Heights. "You're telling me for the first time," Lieutenant William E. Jameson, head of the Maple Heights detective bureau, told the *Plain Dealer*. "If he lives in the area, undoubtedly we'll talk to him."

And there the story, at least the public side of it, ends. The reports detailing the three-month Fuerst–Shankland investigation should be a part of the Beverly Potts files, but when I examined the box of records in the spring of 2003, those official papers were not there. Detective Robert Wolf of the Cleveland Police Department investigated the Beverly Potts case for eighteen months beginning in the summer of 2000, and he similarly acknowledges that the Fuerst-Shankland reports were not part of the Potts files. Considering that the case records contain reports that postdate 1974, the absence of that particular batch of documents seems strange, if not exactly troublesome. Detective Wolf was never able to locate those papers, and his interview with Fuerst yielded little new information and shed no light on the present whereabouts of his and Shankland's reports detailing their three-month investigation into the mysterious Maple Heights child molester.

NOTES

The only existing records dealing with this particular phase of the Potts investigation remain two newspaper articles: one by John P. Coyne in the August 17, 1980, edition of the *Plain Dealer* and a similar (unsigned) piece in the *Press* of August 18. I do not mean to suggest anything sinister by pointing to the absence of the Fuerst–Shankland reports in the Beverly Potts case files. Though massive, the Potts files remain incomplete, and reports far older than those from 1974 are numbered among the missing. When authorities realized the relevance of those documents to the Tiffany Papesh investigation in 1980, it is likely they were removed for study and never returned.

1988

The Pennsylvania Child Killer

The *Plain Dealer* contacted Cleveland police in late January 1988. What
did they know about William Henry Redmond? The paper had picked up
on an Associated Press story from Philadelphia involving the one-time
Ferris wheel operator who had been recently arrested for the April 1951
murder of eight-year-old Jane Marie Althoff in Trainer, Pennsylvania, near
Philadelphia. Long suspected in the brutal killing, Redmond had managed to avoid arrest in the child's death for more than thirty-five years.
Now, seriously ill and bedridden with emphysema, he lay in a Delaware
County, Pennsylvania, jail hooked to an oxygen tank awaiting the justice that would come either from the state or his own ravaged lungs. Was
there any chance, the *Plain Dealer* wanted to know, that the still-unsolved
disappearance of Beverly Potts could be laid at Redmond's feet?

It was more than simply an intriguing possibility. Barely three months
separated the two crimes, and there were other eerie similarities, as well.
Redmond had been employed as a Ferris wheel assembler and operator
by Pennsylvania Premier Shows, and in April 1951 the carnival had set
up shop in Trainer. Jane Marie had gone to the carnival with her two
brothers, Paul and Lamar, on April 25, and witnesses had seen the young
girl talking to Redmond before she inexplicably vanished. Searchers discovered her body the next day in a truck on carnival grounds. Police
found Redmond's fingerprints all over the inside of the vehicle's cab,
but before he could be arrested and questioned, he disappeared without
picking up his final paycheck. Pennsylvania authorities issued a formal
warrant for Redmond's arrest in 1952. A check into his violent past revealed they had good reasons to assume the Ferris wheel operator's guilt.
In November 1935, at the age of thirteen, he had sexually assaulted eight-

year-old Esther Strickland of Conneaut, Ohio. (There is some confusion here. Newspaper accounts mention a second Conneaut victim, though no name is provided. Police reports, however, refer only to Esther Strickland. The confusion is further compounded by a February 25, 1999, article about Redmond in the *Grand Island* [Nebraska] *Independent* [Redmond had lived in Grand Island] by reporter Carol Bryant that makes reference to an October 1935 attack on two preteen girls in Lancaster, Ohio, as well as an attempted rape and assault on a Conneaut preteen in October 1938.) His attack on Esther Strickland had been unspeakably brutal; and, incorrectly assuming he had killed his victim, he piled concrete blocks on her body and left the scene. After his arrest, Redmond was confined to the Boys Industrial School in Lancaster, Pennsylvania. Sometime in either 1938 or 1939, he had been transferred to Lima State Hospital in Mansfield, Ohio, where he remained until 1943. Patrolman Malcolm Murphy of the Pennsylvania State Police had picked up Redmond's cold trail after he and other troopers were assigned in 1985 to clear out some old, unsolved cases. Murphy ran Redmond's name through police computer networks and found him living in Grand Island, Nebraska. In late January 1988 Redmond was arrested and sent back to Pennsylvania where he was arraigned on a nine-count indictment in the 1951 murder of Jane Marie Althoff, including criminal homicide, and held without bail. "We're looking into the possibility that this man might be connected to the murder of Beverly Potts," homicide unit supervisor Sergeant John Fransen told the *Plain Dealer* on January 27, 1988.

By 1988 the erroneous assumption that Beverly Potts had disappeared while she and Patsy Swing had been attending a carnival had become a permanent fixture of Cleveland legend, and Redmond's job as a Ferris wheel operator inevitably revived all those notions of wandering lowlifes with shady pasts who worked traveling circuses and shows. Fransen and Detective Donald Ferris could not find any reference to Redmond in the Potts case files, and though they checked everything from motor-vehicle registrations to utility-company records, they could not find any local documents that would place him in Cleveland during August 1951. The simple passage of time had obscured the path he had taken almost forty years before. There had been a "Home Day" carnival in Brooklyn Village at the time of Beverly's disappearance, but authorities could not link Redmond to it, nor could they place him at Puritas Springs Park, the amusement park on the city's West Side.

But the tantalizing possibility that William Henry Redmond might hold the key to one of Cleveland's most famous and inexplicable mysteries ultimately proved too strong to ignore, so on St. Patrick's Day 1988, two months after the *Plain Dealer's* inquiry, Fransen and Ferris drove to Pennsylvania to question the one-time carnival worker. Lying flat on his back in a hospital bed with his oxygen supply close at hand, Redmond treated the whole affair with a maddening blend of disdain and disinterest. The pair of Cleveland policemen interrogated him for the better part of a day. They showed him Beverly's photograph and did their best to pry some sort of statement out of him; but Redmond remained obstinately passive, steadfastly refusing to admit or deny his guilt. Occasionally, he would reach for his oxygen supply and lapse into total silence as the mask covered his face. Fransen and Ferris dangled a carrot in front of him: all they were interested in, they insisted, was closure for the Potts family. If Redmond was guilty of her murder and admitted as much, no further charges would be brought against him. "Willy! All you have to do is tell us you had nothing to do with Beverly Potts and we're out of here," Ferris cajoled, but Redmond remained grimly silent. Patrolman Murphy stood unobtrusively to one side and watched Redmond's reactions carefully as the two Cleveland cops did their best to get something out of him. When Fransen and Ferris gave up in frustration, Murphy took them aside and assured them that they had found their man; Redmond had reacted to questions about the Jane Marie Althoff killing in exactly the same manner, he insisted. Fransen knew in his gut that he and Ferris had spent the day sparring with the most monstrous sort of serial killer. It was simply impossible to believe that Redmond's roster of brutal assaults stopped with Esther Strickland and Jane Marie Althoff. A predator of such viciousness does not suddenly give up his murderous activities; there had to be other victims for whom Redmond was responsible. But there was no way to prove it, at least not in 1988. Disappointed, frustrated, and empty-handed, Fransen and Ferris returned to Ohio gnawed by the tantalizing possibility they had faced Beverly Potts's killer. "I'd feel better about it if I could have placed him in Cleveland," Fransen reflected recently.

William Henry Redmond managed to maintain his tenuous grip on life for another four years. As the result of an unforgivable series of legal screwups and judicial breakdowns, he eluded trial and never had to face justice for the murder of Jane Marie Althoff; determinedly silent to the

end, he died on January 19, 1992. Today, John Fransen is angry but philosophical, and his instincts—honed by years on the police force—leave
him convinced that Redmond was responsible for far more vicious may-
hem than anyone realized. "I'll tell you what," he remarked. "He's killed
other girls, and Beverly Potts might be one of them." And, indeed, recent revelations would seem to prove the veteran cop correct. In early
1999, seven years after Redmond's death, Lieutenant Tim Sheridan of
the West Bloomfield, Michigan, Police Department began looking into
the March 1955 rape and murder of seven-year-old Barbara Gaca of Detroit. The girl had been on her way to school, six blocks from her home,
when she inexplicably vanished on March 24. Her brutalized body turned
up seven days later in a dump about twenty-five miles away from her
home wrapped in an Army blanket. Sheridan fed thirteen pages of information about the Gaca killing into the FBI's Violent Criminal Apprehension System (VICAP), a database that compares the specific features
of a single violent crime with other similar acts of violence. The search
produced two possible perpetrators: one could be eliminated because
he was serving time in prison at the time of the Barbara Gaca assault;
the other was William Henry Redmond. Sheridan's determined digging
even unearthed yet another killing to which Redmond had been tenta-
tively linked: the September 19, 1949, murder of Joanne Lynn in Lima,
New York. While waiting trial in Pennsylvania for the Jane Marie Althoff
killing, Redmond is alleged to have confessed to a fellow inmate, "They
may have me on this one but not the other three." Just as Ferris and
Fransen had done a decade before, Sheridan tried to link Redmond to
the vicious, still unsolved Barbara Gaca and Joanne Lynn murders by
tracing his movements through his employment history—which included jobs as a carnival truck driver and a Ferris wheel operator, as well
as a stint with the railroads—during that crucial period from the late
1940s to the early 1950s.

Ironically, as determined digging added more possible victims to
Redmond's bloody tally, the less likely it seems he could be responsible
for Beverly Potts's fate. At age ten and tall for her years, Beverly falls
outside the preferred age range of Redmond's usual alleged targets. Seven
or eight would seem to have been his ages of choice. And no trace of
Beverly was ever found; in each of the brutal attacks potentially linked
to Redmond, however, the battered victim had simply been abandoned
or dumped with no real attempt at concealment. No doubt, William

Henry Redmond went to his grave with blood on his hands and secrets in his heart. Could he have been in or around Halloran Park on the night of August 24, 1951? Perhaps. But the answer to that question seems destined to remain a tantalizing riddle within the Beverly Potts mystery.

NOTES

All the information relevant to the investigation into William Henry Redmond is drawn from police reports and notes in the Potts case files. His initial arrest by Pennsylvania authorities is covered by an Associated Press story in the January 27, 1988, issue of the *Plain Dealer* and a piece by Mary Jayn Woge carried the next day. John Fransen supplied additional information when I interviewed him in July 2003. The speculations linking Redmond to the Gaca and Lynn murders, as well as his alleged confession, were reported in a February 1999 article by Carol Bryant in the *Grand Island* (Nebraska) *Independent*.

The Tale of the Murderous Milkman

In February 1994, Michael and Michelle Vacha were renovating a house in Cleveland on Midvale Avenue that they had recently purchased, when they made a startling discovery. As Michael tore up the old carpeting on the stairs, he found a couple of pieces of torn, yellowed notebook paper, a man's shirt, and some other papers hidden under the rubber matting of the third step from the bottom. The two-page note minutely recorded what the writer insisted were the true facts in the kidnapping and death of Beverly Potts. The mysterious document spun out a lurid, indeed horrifying, tale of rape, murder, and dismemberment. The writer identified her husband, Steve, as Beverly's killer. He had been, she alleged, the Potts's milkman; and on one occasion he had brutally raped Elizabeth Potts while making his regular deliveries. Beverly, therefore, was his daughter, not Robert Potts's. The child's death, she insisted, had come about from an accidental drug overdose. The "letter" presented a veritable catalogue of horrors, including terrible odors and blood splatters in the basement, as well as mysterious packages wrapped in brown butcher paper, body parts being burned in the furnace, and murderous threats made by the one-time milkman. The writer revealed that Steve used to drive his family slowly past Halloran Park, laughing menacingly as he did so and joking about the criminal returning to the scene of his crime. He had even attended Elizabeth Potts's 1956 funeral, the letter reported. Subsequently, the letter went on, he was so totally overcome by a fit of uncharacteristic remorse that he began sending money orders to Robert Potts to make up, in part, for the devastation he had caused the family. Immediately after reading the letter, the startled Vacha couple telephoned Cleveland police, and when officers failed to show up in what they deemed a timely fashion, they alerted Channel 5 news. When police did arrive at the Midvale address, they found cameras already rolling and the place crawling with Channel 5 news personnel.

The Vachas had apparently purchased the house from an Anna Haynik, now living in retirement in suburban Kansas City close to her children. She had divorced her husband, Steve, in 1955. The three Haynik children admitted that their late father—who died in 1981 while living in Florida—was hardly an exemplary citizen, but balked at the notion that he could be involved in the kidnapping and murder of Beverly Potts. Although wanting to avoid unfavorable publicity and to protect their mother from any unnecessary emotional strain, the Haynik children reluctantly agreed to allow her to be interviewed by Cleveland police—but in person, not by phone. In early March, therefore, Detectives Richard Martin and Edward Gray received the necessary official permission and funds to travel to Kansas City. They found an eighty-three-year-old woman seemingly frightened, confused, forgetful, and, perhaps, even evasive. Under Martin's and Gray's gentle but persistent questioning over a five-hour period, however, Anna Haynik finally admitted that she had, indeed, written and carefully hidden the incriminating document that the Vachas had found under the stair carpeting—her favorite hiding place—in her former home, but insisted that none of the allegations were true. It was all an elaborate hoax, a revenge plot aimed at her abusive husband. By 1953, Mrs. Haynik had grown so terrified of her husband that she feared he would kill her and their three children, so she concocted an elaborate story patched together from pieces of the news reports dealing with Beverly's disappearance and grisly details culled from detective novels. She acknowledged hiding the incriminating letter implicating her husband, Steve, in the Potts affair where the Vachas had found it, hoping that if he did, indeed, murder her, the document would ultimately be found, thus giving her the last laugh from beyond the grave. Mrs. Haynik sheepishly informed Detectives Martin and Gray that she had simply forgotten about it. "She was remorseful about it and embarrassed," Martin told the *Plain Dealer* on March 8, 1994. "It's not something she was proud of, but in the marriage and situation she was in, it was her only alternative." It seems that Anna Haynik's creativity did not end with the disappearance of Beverly Potts; she also put together, she admitted, an elaborate fiction implicating her husband, along with Dr. Sam Sheppard, in the 1954 murder of Marilyn Sheppard. The fate of that particular document remains unknown.

NOTES

The story of the letter's discovery and all subsequent events are contained in police reports from the relevant period, February–March, 1994. The Vacha-Haynik incident was also covered in a pair of *Plain Dealer* articles: one by Mark Gillispie in the February 26, 1994 issue, the other by Douglas Montero carried in the March 8 edition.

Bones in the Basement

Detective Michaelene M. Taliano of the Cleveland Police Department winced. The elderly woman prefaced her story with a phrase cops have come to distrust and loath: "Please don't think I'm crazy, but . . . " But this time it was different; now nearing the end of her life, the woman meticulously unfolded a compelling tale that had, she lamented, been weighing on her mind for years, one that would eventually take police and three bone-sniffing German shepherds to the basement of a house on Graber Drive in Lakewood for a glamorously laden exercise in up-to-date crime detection. Yet another act in the long-running, seemingly endless tragedy of Beverly Potts was about to play itself out, and the source again would be an aggrieved wife. The woman had, she recounted, been locked in a loveless marriage with an alcoholic whom she both feared and distrusted, and a series of circumstances over the years had led her to the chilling conclusion that her husband bore responsibility for the death of Beverly Potts. If Detective Taliano had access to the Potts case files, the woman was sure she would find his name mentioned. She clearly remembered the day nearly fifty years before when a couple of policemen came to the house and grilled her husband about his possible connection to the disappearance of the little girl from Linnet Avenue. The woman then directed the startled detective to her in-laws' former home on Graber Drive. Her husband's parents were, she insisted, the sort of people who would support their son in anything. She would not put covering up a crime beyond them, and she clearly remembered their having a wall built in their basement at the time of Beverly's disappearance. Her body was, she speculated, either concealed behind that wall or in the crawl space at the front of the house.

Though they willingly offered their full cooperation, Detective Taliano laughs when she remembers the startled, incredulous look on the present owners' faces when she presented herself at their door with an official request to have a look at their basement. She and her partner, Detective George Stitt, watched carefully as each of the three bone-sniffing dogs supplied by the Ohio Search Dog Association was released individually to explore the basement near the now almost fifty-year-old wall and the crawl space. Without exception, each dog showed a marked interest in the northeast corner; in fact, one of the shepherds, according to Taliano, went "absolutely bonkers." Police dug down about a foot in the spot that had attracted so much sophisticated canine attention, unearthing a lace-up boot, easily a century or more old, and a scattering of bones. Could these long-buried bits of skeleton be the remains of Beverly Potts? But when the bones turned out to be from an animal, or animals, police brass unceremoniously pulled the plug on the entire operation without further explanation. Were those few animal bones sufficient to explain the intense reactions of three highly trained dogs? Could there have been other bones buried farther down? The unfortunate termination of the search leaves those questions unanswered.

NOTES

The police reports detailing this incident are filed with other documents relevant to Beverly Potts's disappearance. Detective Michaelene Taliano (now retired) provided further information during an interview on June 4, 2003.

Anniversaries

Cleveland's newspapers chose to remember Beverly Potts at odd intervals. On the sixth, seventh, and tenth anniversaries of her now-legendary disappearance, the press reminded city residents of the little girl who vanished so completely and inexplicably from their midst on the evening of August 24, 1951. Reporters returned to Linnet Avenue and interviewed individuals from the dwindling pool of playmates and neighbors who had lived on the street when the tragedy unfolded in such a glare of media attention. Though specific memories were inevitably fading, it seemed everyone who had known her, both children and adults, had something to share about Beverly Potts. Fears of Halloran Park, especially at night, still lingered; and watchful parents would use Beverly's tragic example to compel curfew obedience from successive generations of neighborhood youngsters. Inevitably, local old-timers and those new to the neighborhood would sit on their front porches, stare into the twilight, and think about those painful events from long ago every year as August 24 approached. The sight of Robert Potts, now living alone in the small house that had once sheltered a family of four and a host of relatives, always conjured up memories of and musings about his missing daughter. Aging, still employed at the Allen Theater, and determinedly silent, he rarely spoke of Beverly and enjoyed only minimal, though friendly, contact with his neighbors. Inevitably, newspapermen cracked whatever shell of privacy he had managed to form around himself every time a new memorial piece about Beverly was in the offing. "I wish you'd forget about it. I'm trying to," he grumbled to *Plain Dealer* reporter Pat Garling on August 24, 1958. But Cleveland neither would nor could forget the little girl from Linnet Avenue. On August 23, 2003—the fifty-second anniversary, minus one day, of her disappearance—Robert Wolf,

Doris O'Donnell Beafait, and I were in the Linnet Avenue-Halloran Park neighborhood, along with personnel from Storytellers Media Group, tapping a documentary about the city's most famous missing child. Three youngsters, the oldest certainly no more than seven or eight, glided up to us on their bicycles as we prepared for a take. Suspiciously, they surveyed us and our equipment. "What are you doing?" asked the senior member of the group, his childish curiosity mixed with a certain sense of proprietorship about his neighborhood. Producer-director Mark Stone bent over and patiently answered: "We're making a movie about a little girl who used to live here and disappeared a long time ago." The junior inquisitor regarded him knowingly and replied without hesitation, "The one who got kidnapped at Halloran!"

The press also reminded Clevelanders about Beverly Potts whenever another local child, especially a girl close to her age, was kidnapped or murdered. When seven-year-old Renaldo B. Goldsby and his six-year-old cousin Virgil G. Stone inexplicably disappeared while on an errand from the Goldsby residence on East 140 Street on New Year's Day 1973, the *Plain Dealer* compared the two missing boys to Beverly Potts. When a never-apprehended-or-identified predator murdered Beverly Jarosz of Garfield Heights in 1965 and in 1980 when Tiffany Papesh mysteriously vanished from a Maple Heights convenience store close to her home, the press recalled Beverly Potts and searched for the obvious points of comparison between the cases. And comparisons were made with other cases: eight-year-old Arthur Noske, beaten to death by his mother's boyfriend in 1977; fourteen-year-old Tammy Seals, killed by Orlando Morales in 1981 while she was delivering morning newspapers; fourteen-year-old Angela Hicks, her nude body found in a wooded area in Elyria, Ohio, a month after her stepfather reported her missing in 1990. In mid-September 2003, as described earlier, eleven-year-old Shakira Johnson suddenly vanished from a block party at East 106 Street and Benham Avenue. A month later an anonymous phone tip led police to an abandoned warehouse on East 71 Street, where her mutilated body lay in the underbrush. Cleveland mourned; the *Plain Dealer* remembered. The paper solemnly added Shakira's name to the city's grim tally of murdered and missing children. Topping the melancholy list was the missing little girl from Linnet Avenue—her fate still a perplexing mystery after more than half a century. Cleveland would never memorialize Beverly Potts with an "Amber Alert" or a "Megan's Law," but she had become a local symbol for all missing children, and her case the yardstick by which the circumstances of all other child abductions and murders were measured. Invariably, on these memorial occasions, the press reminded city readers what Beverly had looked like by reprinting one of the few photographs of her remaining in newspaper files. There she was again as Cleveland had always seen her—the same Mona Lisa smile, the same wide-set dark eyes. Was it a trick of the photography or of the imagination that made those eyes seem so moving, so haunting? Like a heavily retouched portrait of an old Hollywood star, those photos of Beverly seemed to belong to another age. As a new millennium dawned, the fiftieth anniversary of her disappearance loomed on the horizon. It was the summer of the year 2000, and a new, wrenching chapter in the ongoing drama of the missing little girl from Linnet Avenue was about to open.

Robert Wolf's Quest

If he wandered into his backyard and stole into its extreme southwest corner, he could look diagonally across into that other backyard—the empty, lonely one where no children ever played. Sometimes he could catch a glimpse of the grim, silent old man who lived alone in the small, dark house. To Bobby Wolf, he was a little "spooky," but he felt sorry for him—as much sorrow as any five-year-old boy could summon for a grown-up to whom he had never spoken. That was her father—the father of the little girl who had once played in that now deserted backyard years before he had even been born, the lost little girl who had left her house one evening long ago and had never come home. Everyone in the neighborhood, including his parents, still talked about her—still warned their own children that her unhappy fate might befall them if they weren't careful and home before dark; and though it was now the mid-1960s, that little girl's presence was palpable. She was as real as the children with whom Bobby walked to Louis Agassiz Elementary School, as real as the friends with whom he romped at Halloran Park. He had no idea what she looked like, and it would be years before he ever saw her photograph. But her face drifted in the evening air on cool fall days and sometimes flickered softly behind the curtains when he walked by and glanced furtively at the house on Linnet Avenue. His awareness of her had no clear beginning; he seemed to have absorbed her tragic story just as he had the sight of his parents' faces hovering over his crib. Robert Wolf spent his childhood with Beverly Potts, and she would follow him into his adulthood.

On July 13, 2000, detective Robert Wolf, a decorated, fifteen-year veteran of the Cleveland Police Force working out of the First District, reported as ordered to chief Martin Flask's office. Wolf had worked a number of

Ex-Cleveland Police detective Robert Wolf and the author at Halloran Park in spring 2003, tracing Beverly's movements and reconstructing the events of August 24, 1951. Photo by Denise Blanda.

difficult, time-consuming assignments—small but complicated details related to ongoing cases. Consequently, he had developed a reputation in the department for what he dubs *"Mission Impossible* jobs," and he assumed Flask intended to hand him another brain buster. The chief motioned Wolf over to the conference table in his office and got right to the point: "What, if anything, do you know about the Beverly Potts case?"

Later that afternoon, Wolf sat in the department's forensic lab scrutinizing a strange letter. "To Whom it may Concern," it began. The handwriting was shaky, cramped, virtually collapsed in upon itself, and exceedingly difficult to read, but as Wolf labored through the first sentence, the wan and ghostly face from his boyhood, the one that had sometimes floated by the windows of that house on Linnet Avenue, came back to him. "Now that I am in the twilight of my life nearing my 82nd year of age I will tell what happened to Beverly Potts." The letter had arrived at the editorial offices of the *Plain Dealer* the day before, on July 12. One of the paper's employees responsible for opening and sorting through the mountains of correspondence that routinely pour into *Plain Dealer* offices immediately brought it to Brent Larkin's attention. Larkin (director of the paper's editorial pages) called Chief Flask, and within a few hours, a small contingent of plainclothes officers picked up the mysterious letter and delivered it to police headquarters. Wolf smiled inwardly as he read; he had once joked with his wife, "The next thing they'll give me is the Beverly Potts case." The anonymous writer confessed to killing the ten-year-old girl by accident on the night of August 24, 1951, at Edgewater Park and to disposing of her body by tossing it from the "high level bridge" into the Cuyahoga River, where—the writer assumed—it was ultimately carried out to Lake Erie and lost. "I only wanted to fondle her," the writer admitted. "But she started screaming & yelling fearing that someone would hear her I hit her with my fist and she went limp."

It was an intriguing tale and certainly a plausible solution to the fifty-year-old mystery, but it was impossible to check out any of the details. Wolf was also perplexed. All sorts of inaccuracies and questionable assertions hobbled the writer's confessional narrative. Perhaps because Harvey Lee Rush had insisted in December 1955 that he had abducted a little girl from a "circus," the nature of the entertainment at Halloran that night has gradually metamorphosed from simple Showagon to full-blown carnival, complete with rides, calliope, and makeshift midway. The abductor and murderer thus becomes a roving lowlife who eked out a meager living as a carnival worker—someone who could lure Beverly by taking advantage of her naivete and fascination with performing. All the newspaper and police reports at the time of Beverly's disappearance, however, correctly maintained that she and Patsy Swing had gone to a Showagon performance. That she disappeared from a carnival or circus remains one of the most enduring misconceptions about the Beverly Potts legend, and the mysterious writer was perpetuating that error. "They [Beverly and Patsy] were watching some carnival workers [possibly 'monkeys'] who were erecting [or, perhaps, 'bracing'] rides at the park." The writer asserted, "She was very friendly and I had no trouble getting her in my car that was parked nearby." The story just did not make sense. It is not just a matter of Beverly's parents insisting she was too shy to be lured by or even talk to a stranger. By all accounts—her teachers, her friends, everyone who knew her—Beverly was not just shy; she was very shy, especially around men and boys. One acquaintance even went so far as to call her "backward." When Detective Wolf later questioned Patricia Swing, she firmly rejected the writer's contention that Beverly would have been easy for a stranger to talk with and further insisted she simply would not talk to a stranger at all. Therefore, all the various contemporary reports of her speaking to a man or men in a dark car or accepting a ride home become hard to swallow—even if she did know one of them; and the mysterious letter writer was maintaining he had no trouble striking up a conversation with her and luring her into his automobile.

The oddest allegation in this questionable confession concerned the manner in which the author actually determined he had accidentally killed Beverly. "I thought I had only knocked her out but after fondling her for a few minutes she was getting pretty cold." A few minutes? It would take hours for a dead body to cool down sufficiently so as to be cold to the touch.

It would have been easy for Wolf to dismiss the curious missive as the work of a crank. For one thing, the letter was absolutely devoid of any emotion; it read more like a report than a confession. But what could possibly motivate someone who—by all appearances—seemed to be elderly and infirm to confess, however inaccurately, to a fifty-year-old crime? Was there a catalyst of some kind somewhere that could have spurred the unidentified correspondent into this peculiar action? Whoever the author was, he did seem to command a certain basic knowledge of the Potts case. In spite of the factual errors and questionable assertions, was he confessing to a crime he had committed, or thought he had committed, in his past? Even someone else's crime? Were the inaccuracies the simple product of compromised mental faculties or was the writer trying to protect his identity even as he confessed? Or was he simply perpetrating a hoax? Before leaving Flask's office, Wolf found himself detailed to the homicide unit—an official action a notch below a permanent transfer. "See if you can find out who wrote it," Flask had ordered. "Give it ninety days!" But ninety days would stretch out to almost eighteen months; and the task of identifying the anonymous sender would pull Wolf into the murky depths of the unknown writer's mind and ultimately lead him to an old box of police files, where he took up the musty, tangled threads of an abandoned investigation nearly half a century old.

Potential evidence is potential evidence; it doesn't matter whether the crime is fifty minutes or fifty years old. The writer had spelled "Linnet" correctly and had also properly designated the street as "Ave.," rather than "Street" or "Road." Small points, perhaps, but potentially significant in assessing the reliability of someone who was claiming he had he lived in the area at the time of Beverly's disappearance. The letter had been postmarked on July 11, 2000, the day before its arrival at the *Plain Dealer* offices. The stamp had been out of circulation for a year and was of a type that had been sold only at Huntington and FirstStar banks. It had been cancelled at Cleveland's central post office, so there was no way of determining from where in the county the letter had been mailed. DNA tests of the envelope flap at the Cuyahoga County Morgue indicated the writer to be male. Checks for latent fingerprints on the envelope and letter proved negative. Either the writer had been extremely careful, or perhaps he was truly as old as the shaky, erratic penmanship would suggest. (An elderly person with extremely dry skin would not easily leave fingerprints behind.) If the piece of paper on which the letter had been composed had come from a tablet of some sort, then impressions of what had been written on the sheet directly above it could be lifted. But that test proved negative as well. Though handwriting analysis by the Cleveland Police Department indicated that the author was, indeed, up in years, Wolf remained uncertain. The writer could be intentionally trying to disguise his handwriting, writing with his off hand, or even writing on the hood of an idling pickup truck.

And why now? If the writer had truly been living for almost fifty years with the murder of Beverly Potts weighing on his conscience, what had prompted him to this bizarre act of confession at this particular moment? The answer to that question could point Detective Wolf in the direction of the author, perhaps even Beverly Potts's killer. The *Plain Dealer* had published local freelance writer Fred Mcgunagle's lengthy retrospective on the Potts case in the Editorials and Forum section on Saturday, January 23, 1999. But that had been more than seventeen months earlier—far too long a period to serve as the catalyst for this piece of correspondence. Wolf located the potential trigger in—of all places—the *Plain Dealer* obituaries of July 11, 2000. "Margaret 'Peg' Kilbane, Veteran Police Sergeant," read the lead. The one-time member of the Cleveland Police Department's former Women's Bureau had retired in 1972 and died in her eighty-eighth year. A short paragraph toward the top of the obit immediately drew Wolf's attention. "In 1951, she spent more than six months investigating the disappearance of Beverly Potts, a 10-year-old who vanished from a carnival [*sic*] at Halloran Park a block from her West Side home. Nearly 50 years later, the case remains unsolved." By then, Wolf had labored through most of the surviving police reports at least once and had gathered all the contemporary coverage from Cleveland's three dailies. The name Margaret Kilbane simply did not appear at all in the press and very rarely in official documents. (I located only two reports that referred to her—one simply in passing, the other detailing her role as a decoy in an attempt to snag a sick extortionist at the May Company.) Contrary to what her tribute suggested, Sergeant Kilbane's involvement in the Potts case was rather minimal. The obituary had run on the morning of July 11; the writer had actually composed and sent his mysterious letter later that same day. What was there about the Kilbane obituary that had apparently antagonized him? Was he someone—a retired policeman, perhaps—familiar enough with the Potts investigation to take offense at the seemingly undeserved posthumous credit the late sergeant was getting?

On Thursday, August 24, 2000, the forty-ninth anniversary of Beverly Potts's disappearance, the *Plain Dealer* published a memorial piece by Brent Larkin in the Metro section of the paper. "Forty-nine years ago today," he began, "the little girl Greater Clevelanders can't forget slipped into history." "Although the case eventually disappeared from the headlines," Larkin concluded, "Cleveland police would continue receiving information about Beverly for decades. To this day, they investigate all tips regarding her disappearance." Detective Wolf waited patiently on the sidelines to see if the mysterious letter writer would respond in some way to Brent Larkin's anniversary remembrance. Two weeks passed, but he remained silent. Meanwhile, Wolf tried to narrow the search for the still-elusive author. But he was working alone without any backup support or even secretarial help, and he faced a job so massive it would have taxed the combined efforts of Sherlock Holmes, Perry Mason, and James Bond. Wolf operated on the assumption that the elderly writer still lived, probably alone, in or near the Linnet Avenue neighborhood. After gathering together lists of stamp purchases from Huntington and FirstStar ATMs in the area, voter-registration records, DMV records, and *Plain Dealer* subscription lists, he began cross-checking the incredibly long and imposing documents, looking for a name, any name, that occurred more than once. Compared to this laborious, Hail-Mary effort, looking for the proverbial needle in the haystack was child's play.

During the second week of September, Larkin interviewed Wolf about the July 12 letter's official odyssey, after it had been turned over to Cleveland police. Local authorities and the *Plain Dealer's* editorial staff had kept the piece of correspondence secret, but on Saturday, September 9, Larkin broke the story to the public. "At The Plain Dealer, we receive dozens of letters each year from residents of the state and federal prison systems imploring us to right a wrong by investigating their convictions," he wrote. "We generally don't receive letters that amount to confessions. But on the afternoon of July 12, we did. In that day's mail came a hand-written letter, postmarked from Cleveland a day earlier, confessing to one of the most famous unsolved crimes in the city's history: The disappearance of Beverly Potts." After a brief recap of the fifty-year-old Potts tragedy, Larkin told Clevelanders that police were taking the letter seriously. "We have been actively pursuing any and all leads associated with this letter," Detective Wolf insisted. "This includes analyzing forensic evidence that the writer of the letter mistakenly overlooked." Larkin left his readers with the tantalizing suggestion that the strange letter might hold the key to the Potts mystery. "Solving a 49-year-old crime would be almost unprecedented. Solving it by means of a letter written and sent by the killer's own hand would be simply amazing."

This time the mysterious correspondent rose from the shadows to take the bait. "Dear Mr. Larkin," his second letter began in the same crabbed, cramped handwriting as the first. "As doctors don't give me very long to live I have left a letter with my lawyer to be opened in the event of my death." The writer followed this tantalizing piece of information with the same cryptic combination of intriguing assertions and strange inaccuracies that had characterized his initial letter. He alleged that his conscience had gotten the better of him as far back as 1967 and that, consequently, he had written to coroner Sam Gerber asking him to arrange some sort of plea-bargain agreement for manslaughter on his behalf with then Cuyahoga County Prosecutor John T. Corrigan. "Mr. Gerber could have had this case cleared up 33 years ago but he chose not to," lamented the writer. "Now arthritis and cancer and diabetes have taken over my body and I will be in the Riverside Cemetery before another year is out." He closed his latest epistle with the startling assertion that the envelope in the possession of his attorney contained "a 1916 Liberty Standing Quarter"—an extraordinarily rare and valuable coin—that he insisted Beverly had carried with her in a coin purse on the night of August 24, 1951.

Wolf immediately had both envelope and letter checked for fingerprints; again, the results were negative. This time, however, there was no DNA evidence on the envelope flap. Perhaps Wolf's reference to "forensic evidence that the writer of the letter mistakenly overlooked" in Larkin's September 9 piece had spooked him. In an extraordinarily bizarre and cautious maneuver, the author had sealed the envelope with pieces of scotch tape that had been removed from the dispenser with a rusty pair of pliers; flecks of rust still adhered to the adhesive side of the tape, and the imprints of the tool were readily apparent. Wolf regarded this most recent epistle with the same mixture of fascination and perplexity that had marked his response to the first. Even to the untrained eye, the handwriting in the two pieces of correspondence was identical—a significant detail that the FBI would later verify; and since it would be virtually impossible to fake such penmanship so convincingly twice in a row, Wolf now accepted as fact that the writer was, indeed, an elderly man. But this second letter seriously complicated an already difficult investigation. "I wanted to vomit," Wolf remarked to me. "It [the second letter] added all kinds of additional variables to the equation that I had to check out." The attorney mentioned was specifically referred to as "she," and the reference to Riverside Cemetery indicated familiarity with Cleveland geography. Again, however, the details just did not add up. None of the original accounts of Beverly's disappearance, either official or unofficial, had mentioned a coin purse; and it seemed utter nonsense to assume she would have had such a rare coin with her when all contemporary sources that even mentioned this small detail agreed she had left the nickel she had earned from washing the supper dishes at home. At least Wolf could pursue the writer's startling allegation that he had written Sam Gerber thirty-three years ago; if true, there would have to be some sort of paper trail. But a search of Gerber's and Corrigan's files turned up nothing, and none of the one-time coroner's or prosecutor's associates with whom Wolf spoke could remember such a potentially significant incident. On one hand, it just did not make sense that the writer would contact the coroner rather than the prosecutor directly; but, on the other hand, even if he had, Gerber's legal training would have prompted him to at least turn such a request over to Corrigan's office or to David Kerr, still serving in the Cleveland Police Department in 1967 and someone whom the coroner knew very well. Gerber's behavior could be erratic and strange at times, but it is simply inconceivable that the coroner would sit on such a potentially important piece of evidence in such a high profile case.

On Sunday, April 8, 2001, Brent Larkin wrote another story, "A new chapter in the case that won't end," in the editorial section of the *Plain Dealer*. Again, Larkin interviewed Wolf for his piece, but this time the detective assumed center stage. "If this person did something terribly wrong nearly 50 years ago, he now has a chance to right that wrong, if these are really amongst his last days on earth. . . . It's time for us—and for the author—to close this sad chapter in Cleveland history. We owe it to the city. And more importantly, we owe it to the memory of Beverly Potts." Cuyahoga County Prosecutor Bill Mason had assured Wolf that because of the writer's advanced age and illnesses, he—assuming he turned out to be Beverly's killer—would most likely be sentenced to a secure, assisted-living facility rather than a conventional state prison, an assurance Wolf passed on in Larkin's piece. He also provided a phone number and urged the writer to contact him. "To this day, many of them [Beverly's friends and family] still hurt over her disappearance and miss her dearly. They want nothing more than for this case to be resolved so they can bring closure to it."

Within a week, the mystery writer responded with an extraordinarily melodramatic announcement: "If I am still living August 24th [the fiftieth anniversary of Beverly's disappearance] I will turn myself in at halloran park at 12 noon. . . . I would like for you [Larkin] to be there with the police Dept. . . . Fifty years is long enough to live with what I have done." For some unfathomable reason, he ignored Detective Wolf's plea to contact him directly, either through the mail or by telephone, and instead again addressed his third letter to Brent Larkin at the *Plain Dealer*. This latest bit of correspondence was somewhat shorter than the other two, and the author's handwriting had deteriorated noticeably. The same disdain for proper punctuation that had characterized his previous communications marked this one as well. Interestingly, August 24 is referred to twice, and on both occasions the writer seems to have initially made a mistake. Whatever number he may have first written (it's difficult to tell whether it is intended to be "7" or "9"), he had crossed it out and written a "4" above. The writer also seemed particularly preoccupied with Brent Larkin. Not only had the letter been addressed to him, the writer specifically wanted Larkin at Halloran Park on the fiftieth anniversary of Beverly's disappearance. The police are brought in almost as an afterthought, and Detective Wolf—though he is a main focus in Larkin's articles of September 9, 2000, and April 8, 2001—is not specifically mentioned. Could the writer be an old, one-time newspaper man appealing to a brother reporter; or, perhaps, a criminal trying to avoid a savvy cop on his tail? Or maybe just a sick prankster who felt he had a better shot at publicity through Brent Larkin and the *Plain Dealer?*

The letter writer may have ignored Detective Wolf's request to either write or call, but approximately one hundred Clevelanders dialed the number of the cell phone Wolf always carried with him. Most calls came from people who still lived with vivid impressions of the Potts case and wanted to share them with a sympathetic ear; a couple came from people who had had close brushes with a similar fate and wanted to get those memories off their chests; many came from cranks. Wolf estimates that about 10 percent of the calls he received actually provided anything useful.

Wolf read and reread the three letters over and over again, literally countless times, looking for any telltale sign—curious word usage, a passing reference of some sort—anything that could point the way to the still anonymous writer. "I was beginning to go nuts," he told me quite matter-of-factly as he paced back and forth in his dining room. "When I was having dinner with my wife and kids, I was thinking about Beverly Potts; when I was playing catch with my son in the yard, I was thinking about this case; when I went to bed at night, I dreamed about the case." The more he delved into the trio of texts, the more he tried to sort out the maddeningly inaccurate assertions, the more convinced he became that this individual—whoever he may have been—was far more than a casual trickster out to create attention for himself by drumming up renewed interest in one of Cleveland's most notorious unsolved cases. Gradually over time, he began to sense dim but familiar echoes from the history of the Potts affair in the writer's assertions, statements in the letters that rang vague bells in his mind. Suddenly, it all came together. The writer actually seemed to be building his elaborate scenario from bits and pieces of the Potts case that had already proven to be hoaxes— details that only someone familiar with the history of the Potts investigation would even know. The reference to the "carnival" at Halloran Park in the first letter recalled Harvey Lee Rush's allusion to a "circus" in his 1955 confession; the writer's insistence that Beverly had been easy to talk with and lure away similarly echoed Rush's tale. In his first letter to the *Plain Dealer*, the anonymous correspondent confessed to Beverly's murder by writing, "But she started screaming & yelling fearing [*sic*] that someone would hear her I hit her with my fist and she went limp." According to the *News* on December 12, 1955, Rush confessed in the following words: "She started crying. . . . I tried to shut her up but she wouldn't stop crying. I then hit her once with my fist. . . . She fell over." On the same day, the *Press* quoted Rush as alleging, "We both sat down and the girl started to cry. I slapped her and she fell over backwards." The *Plain Dealer* gave its version of events without quoting Rush directly: "There, [under a bridge] he said, he slugged her with his fists when she began to scream."

And there was more. Rush had stated he had tried to turn himself in to Detective McArthur but had been rebuffed by police; the anonymous writer alleged that in 1967 he had tried to arrange a plea-bargain agreement through Sam Gerber but had been similarly ignored. In 1953 there had been the sixteen-year-old boy who insisted he would only share his information about Beverly Potts with authorities if they signaled their willingness to grant him protection by reading the cryptic message at the end of NBC's *Dragnet;* the letter writer similarly had asked Gerber to signal his acceptance of the writer's demands by placing an ad in the newspapers. The writer's references to the past events in the Potts case even seemed to include Frank Davis's November 1951 extortion attempt. Davis had concluded one of his calls to Robert Potts with, "God bless you"; the writer signed off in his second letter to Brent Larkin with, "Best wishes to you." Though the writer's preoccupation in his second letter with the "1916 Liberty Standing Quarter," he alleged he had taken from Beverly (one that he insisted he still possessed) had no obvious counterpart in the actual Potts case history, Wolf found an echo in another old case, one in which a special quarter had played a crucial role: the brutal 1948 murder of eight-year-old Sheila Ann Tuley. Again, Wolf wondered: was it even remotely possible that the still unidentified and elusive writer might be a retired cop?

If the writer kept his word, it could all be over on August 24, 2001, the fiftieth anniversary of Beverly Potts's disappearance. All those perplexing questions could be answered, and Beverly's family and friends would finally be granted some kind of closure. But it was not to be. On August 7, 2001—seventeen days before the case's fiftieth anniversary—Brent Larkin received a fourth letter. In the four months since the third piece of correspondence (mailed on April 16), the handwriting had continued to deteriorate alarmingly, and this particular letter was, by far, the shortest of the four. "Sorry I won't be able to keep the appointment on the 24th," he wrote. "I was going to give myself up at the fire station at Halloran park at 12 noon[.] I have to go in a nursing home as I can't keep going on by myself. I have already lived longer than doctors gave me to live." The brief letter was simply, perhaps tauntingly, signed, "your friend."

But this extremely disappointing turn of events did not end the case for Detective Wolf. As the fiftieth anniversary of Beverly's disappearance approached, he checked recent admissions at area nursing homes and searched the *Plain Dealer* obituaries for someone who had died in

The fourth of the so-called Larkin letters. Courtesy of Brent Larkin, the *Plain Dealer*, and Robert Wolf.

his early-to-mid-eighties and was slated for burial in Riverside Cemetery. As Friday, August 24, neared, Wolf knew he could not let the day go by without going to Halloran Park on the admittedly slim chance that the writer might keep his appointment. In the morning, he called Brent Larkin and told him he was on his way to Halloran, back to the neighborhood of his youth. "Neighborhoods like that don't change much—except for the ownership," Anita Potts mused recently; and for the entire day, Wolf silently revisited the familiar playground, Linnet Avenue, and the nearby streets. And, indeed, very little had changed. Some of the houses bore the obvious ravages of time and neglect, but everything looked rather as it did when Robert Wolf was a boy as well as when Beverly was alive. He walked through the park several times, keeping an eye out for any elderly man who seemed more than usually interested in the broad, open expanse; he drove an undercover car slowly through the neighborhood, parked it in a few unobtrusive spots, and watched. If an old man drove by heading toward Halloran, Wolf wrote down the license plate number; he followed the elderly people who ambled down Linnet Avenue with his eyes. He walked into the bar at the southeast corner of West 117 and Linnet—the bar that had stood on the same spot fifty years ago—and checked out the few regulars hanging out there at midday. Though a teetotaler, he ordered a beer and sat at one of the tables trying to pick up pieces of the hushed conversations going on around him. "I didn't want to sit there drinking milk and eating cookies," he joked. He studied the faces in the dark room looking for any telltale hint that signaled anything out of the ordinary. Occasionally, he rose and strolled to the window to check the street and the park. For a while, he tailed a couple of old men who strolled down West 117. Nothing. As the day drew to a close, Wolf surveyed the empty playground and the quiet streets for the last time. This was the fiftieth anniversary of the tragic event that had indelibly scared the neighborhood and the people who had lived there—indeed, the entire city of Cleveland; and still no one really knew exactly what had happened. Visitors to old battlefields often say that if they listen carefully, they can still hear the faint clash of arms; it's part of the atmosphere of the place. On this melancholy anniversary, Wolf did not have to be a psychic to feel the heavy sadness that lingered on Linnet Avenue. It wasn't necessary for him to believe in ghosts to sense the excited murmurs of the large crowd that gathered at Halloran Park a half century ago—or to catch a hint of a little girl's footsteps on the street and sidewalk. When did the sound of those footsteps stop? Where was she when it happened? How close was she to the security of her home?

Brent Larkin was furious. Two days later, on Sunday, August 26, he vented his anger in the Forum section of the *Plain Dealer:* "An Anniversary, a Broken Promise," he wrote. The fact that the anonymous writer had promised in his third letter of April 16, 2001, to surrender himself to police at Halloran Park on the fiftieth anniversary of Beverly Potts's disappearance had been wisely kept from the public for obvious reasons. "But now it doesn't matter," Larkin wrote in disgust. "That's because it is now more likely than ever before that this letter-writing campaign [which had been going on for a year] is nothing more than a hoax perpetuated by someone playing a cruel game with the memory of a 10-year-old girl missing for half a century. . . . It's time to write this guy off as just another in a long line of nuts who have claimed over the years to have been responsible for the longest-running whodunit in the city's history."

Wolf was disappointed but philosophical. "I thought that closure was finally going to come for the Potts family and friends who have suffered over Beverly's disappearance for 50 years," he reflected in Larkin's piece. But he wasn't ready to give up. He continued to check admission records in local nursing homes and to scan the obits in the *Plain Dealer,* looking for some sign that the writer had died. Brent Larkin did not receive any more letters in the now-familiar, almost illegible hand; and, of course, the promised envelope from the female attorney containing a detailed account of what had actually happened to Beverly Potts and the rare quarter never arrived. When I first met Bob Wolf in the winter of 2003, I asked him if he thought the letter writer was dead. Perhaps somewhat reluctantly, he acknowledged that he probably was; and whatever secrets he had been guarding, whatever twisted impulses had prompted him, had died with him.

NOTES

The information in this chapter is drawn from extensive interviews with Robert Wolf and Brent Larkin, as well as from copies of the four letters themselves and from the relevant *Plain Dealer* articles, all of which were supplied by Brent Larkin. Robert Wolf left the Cleveland Police Department in December 2001.

Through a Glass Darkly:
Shadows from the Past

I still think of her as ten years old. She's still a little girl. It's hard for
me to visualize how she would look today.
Anita Potts in a November 2003 interview with Storytellers Media Group

In the early morning hours of July 4, 1954—close to three years after
Beverly Potts vanished—someone bludgeoned Dr. Sam Sheppard's attractive wife, Marilyn, to death in the bedroom of their wealthy, western-
suburb, Bay Village home. The case had everything a Hollywood script
writer, a pulp novelist—or a crusading newspaper editor—could possibly want: blood, brutality, sex, money—a beautiful young victim preg-
nant with her second child; a dapper, handsome, and intelligent principal suspect crippled by his reputation as a philanderer and by an alibi
that seemed to strain credulity to the breaking point; a sensational trial
that attracted national attention. Cleveland's press establishment, led
by Louis B. Seltzer, turned its attention to a brutal new perplexing crime.
But Beverly Potts was not forgotten; she had been on city front pages
and television screens too long to slip quietly into obscurity. In common parlance, we would simply say her case had been placed temporarily on the back burner.

Seltzer's *Press* had cosponsored—along with the City Recreation Department—the Showagon performance at which Beverly had vanished
on Friday night, August 24, 1951. Perhaps troubled by a sense of guilt,
Seltzer—in a clear display of the raw power he commanded in Cleveland—had pulled strings at the police department and had gotten James
McArthur, head of detectives, assigned to the case by Saturday morning, before there was any real evidence of a kidnapping. By the end of

the following week, before there was any conclusive proof of a murder, David Kerr, chief of homicide, was assigned as well. Seltzer sent his reporters and photographers to Linnet Avenue every day for two weeks, and—not to be outdone—the *Plain Dealer* and the *News* followed his lead. Seltzer editorialized about the Potts case and kept the story on the front pages of the *Press* for weeks. And the city's other two dailies did likewise. Arguably, it was this constant, almost obsessive media attention that gave Beverly Potts a local celebrity granted to no other missing child.

That same celebrity was unfortunately passed on to the other members of the Potts household. Elizabeth Potts never recovered from the trauma of her younger daughter's disappearance. "At the mention of Beverly's name, her eyes would well up in tears," recalls Anita. During the months and years that followed the family tragedy, she rarely left the house because strangers invariably recognized her and constantly referred to her as the mother of the missing Beverly Potts. Over time, she and her husband had given away all of Beverly's toys—the bicycle she had ridden to Halloran Park that fateful evening, her prized cardboard dollhouse. Other mementos of their daughter had been carefully packed away. Whenever authorities found a piece of cloth, a bit of clothing, a shoe—any piece of apparel that even vaguely matched the description of what Beverly had been wearing on the night of August 24, 1951, police officers were at the door asking for a positive identification; whenever events propelled Beverly Potts back into the news, the reporters were at the door asking for comment. Elizabeth Potts's health deteriorated rapidly in the years following Beverly's disappearance. "My mother was devastated," Anita remembers. "Early on, when we had to call the police, my mother was already starting to, I think, decline." By April 1956, she had been hospitalized with a liver ailment. On what would have been Beverly's fifteenth birthday—April 15, 1956—she drafted a letter to the Metropolitan Life Insurance Company in New York inquiring about a policy she and her husband had taken out on their second child in September 1941. "On August 24th, 1951," she wrote, "she [Beverly] disappeared from a park right down our street. The agent said he couldn't do anything about it. We've been paying the premiums right along. You can check with the Cleveland Police Dept. Must we continue paying the premiums?" Elizabeth Potts died less than a month later on May 11, 1956.

For the next fourteen years Robert Potts lived alone in the small house on Linnet Avenue that he and his wife had purchased in 1927. The neighborhood around him inevitably changed as the people who had lived there in 1951 drifted away; his contacts with those few remaining were cordial but fleeting. On the one hand, his decision to stay and endure the silence and the painful memories in the now empty house would seem inexplicable. On the other hand, what else could he do? Whether or not he ever consciously admitted it to himself, to leave would be to close the door decisively and forever on the admittedly remote possibility that Beverly might some day return. He died alone on February 22, 1970, while watching television. It would be several days before the newsboy reported to his father that the papers were piling up on the front porch. When police finally broke into the house, they found Robert Potts slumped over in his chair, dead of heart failure, the TV screen still flickering before him.

For Anita Potts, however, the future proved far rosier. She went on to enjoy the sort of professional life of which most young women in the 1950s could only dream. After her 1951 graduation from Notre Dame College in the Cleveland suburb of South Euclid, she accepted a job with the National Cash Register Company at its Cleveland offices on Euclid Avenue. Shortly after the public frenzy over her younger sister's disappearance quieted down, Anita answered a newspaper ad that the U.S. State Department was looking for qualified individuals to work in the Foreign Service. After what the Potts family had endured, she did not take her decision to leave Cleveland lightly. Counseled by her mother that her father would never consent to her living anywhere but home as long as she remained in Cleveland as a single working woman, Anita reluctantly decided to accept the State Department's offer. "Leaving Cleveland, I think, helped me not to think about it constantly," she told Mark Wade Stone of Storytellers Media Group in November 2003. After five weeks of classes in Washington D.C., her government career took her to posts in Tehran, Addis Ababa, and ultimately Paris, where she served with the U.S. delegation to NATO and the Organization for European Cooperation. After two years in the City of Lights, she felt a nagging need for what she describes as "re-Americanization," so she successfully lobbied her superiors for reassignment to the States. Back in Washington, D.C., Anita met and married a marine in February 1962. Her matron of honor at her wedding was her good friend and classmate from Notre Dame College—and Cleveland's future *Plain Dealer* society columnist—Mary Strassmeyer. After years of the wandering-gypsy military life, Anita and her husband now live in retirement; they enjoy three

Beverly's older sister Anita with her husband, Mr. and Mrs. Robert J. Georges, in November 2003. Photo by Mark Wade Stone of Storytellers Media Group.

children, quite literally spread all over the world, and eight grandchildren, including a set of triplets.

But thoughts of the baby sister whom she would never see grow up have stayed with Anita throughout her life. When her own children began rummaging through family albums and piles of old photographs, they asked about the little girl with the deep-set, haunting eyes. "I didn't make a point of telling them," Anita reflected. "But when they saw the old pictures with Beverly in them, they wanted to know what happened, and I told them." The lingering memories of those painful months back in the fall of 1951 also inevitably affected Anita's relationships with her own three children. "My children say I was too strict as a mother because I was worried about where they were, and I had to know where they were, how to reach them. They were to call me if they were late. I don't think I was too terribly strict," she reflects almost wistfully, "but they do."

Anita Potts made her last melancholy journey to Cleveland when her father died in February 1970. She and her husband cleared out the old house on Linnet Avenue and arranged for its sale through an attorney. While sorting though the accumulated clutter of nearly fifty years,

Anita found her sister's tissue-paper-wrapped, ribbon-entwined braids in a drawer. It had been nearly twenty years earlier, just two months before she vanished, that Beverly had finally convinced her mother to cut her nearly foot-long pigtails so she could wear her hair in bangs. After all, she was growing up; she was ten years old now. Being allowed to wear her hair shorter was like a rite of passage into the dawning of her teenage years. How many times during the five years before her death must Elizabeth Potts have quietly grieved over those carefully braided ropes of her daughter's hair? Anita sent one of the pigtails to Robert Wolf during his 2000–01 investigation; it is currently packed away at the Cuyahoga County morgue to aid in the identification process should Beverly's remains ever be found.

In an unbearably poignant tragedy from which no one involved survived unscarred, Patsy Swing, Beverly's next-door neighbor and best friend—the little girl who left the park early and walked home alone because her mother had told her to be back before dark—emerges as the forgotten victim. Constantly stalked by the press and questioned by the

One of Beverly's braids. Photo by Robert Wolf, courtesy of the Cleveland Police Department.

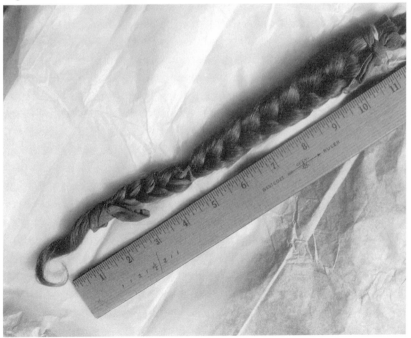

police, repeatedly called "the last person to see Beverly Potts alive," the eleven-year-old child began to crumble under the pressure. There was no way she could avoid seeing the constant parade of well-wishers, relatives, and friends moving in and out of the Potts home next door, where she had been a regular and welcomed visitor; nor could she help but see the police, the reporters, the unending stream of slowly moving cars, the milling crowds during the day, and the more rowdy ones at night. Though her parents did their best to shield her from all the unwanted attention, the Swings reported that their daughter could not eat or sleep. According to a police report dated July 11, 1952, she developed a heart condition. Ultimately, she lost her voice. "Patricia was hospitalized for a time," her mother, Margaret, told *Plain Dealer* reporter Pat Garling on August 24, 1958. "But the doctors were never quite able to determine whether Beverly's disappearance had something to do with her case or not. It may have."

Cleveland knew Patsy Swing through only a single picture taken as part of a series of photographs in the days following her best friend's disappearance and printed in the *News*. It remains probably the most unattractive shot of the group. She is shown standing with her bicycle, hands on the handlebars; the expression on her face seems to suggest boredom, even disgust. It does a distinct disservice to the emotional turmoil with which she was trying to cope.

Living next door to the Potts household must have been impossible for the Swings, even after the public furor over Beverly's disappearance had died down; so on May 3, 1952, Lester Swing moved his family to Parma. Margaret Swing insisted to police in July 1952 that the move had been planned some time before the tragedy because the family found their Linnet Avenue home too small. Patsy graduated from high school, took a job as a telephone operator, married a navy man, and eventually left the state. In late summer of 2002 I spoke with the former Patricia Ann Swing very briefly—long enough, however, to realize that the passing of fifty years has not dulled significantly the edge of her painful memories. "She was my very, very best friend," she asserted, her voice mingling both sadness and defiance. How many times must she have replayed those events of August 24, 1951, in her mind; how many times must she have wondered "What if"—What if she had not left the park and gone home alone that night more than a half century ago? What if she had either stayed with Beverly or insisted more strongly that her friend come home with her? "She shouldn't blame herself," insists Anita

Potts. "It's not her fault. Her mother told her to be home by 9:00, and she was. My mother told Beverly she could stay for the entire show because she loved dancing and music. What if! What if my mother had not let her go?" Indeed, becoming a mother and now a grandmother seems only to have sharpened those troubling thoughts for Patricia Swing. "As long as I don't think about it," she assured me resolutely, "I'm fine!"

I still provoke quizzical, distrustful stares from the locals whenever I wander around Linnet Avenue and Halloran Park. Surely they recognize me by now. I've been drawn there, almost compulsively, so often during the last couple of years. Do the current residents of 11304 think I'm casing their property when they see me so repeatedly on their front sidewalk? Do they know their house's tragic history? Surely they must. A guy with a beard seems to be living next door in the former Swing residence. He has regarded me with deep and evident suspicion several times. Does he know who lived there fifty years ago? Does anyone living on Linnet Avenue now realize their quiet street was barricaded and turned into a madhouse back in 1951? As the summer of 2004 approached, tragic events on Cleveland's West Side again turned a grim spotlight on that old city neighborhood. On April 2, 2004, fourteen-year-old Gina DeJesus vanished from West 105 Street and Lorain Avenue on her way home from Wilbur Wright Middle School. Almost exactly a year before, on April 21, 2003, seventeen-year-old Amanda Berry inexplicably disappeared from the same general area. Their smiling faces appeared in city papers and flashed across local TV screens; reporters began to speak darkly of the "Bermuda Triangle" along Lorain Avenue from which both girls had vanished in less than a year. At the southwest end of that melancholy geometric pattern, Linnet Avenue and Halloran Park still cast their haunting shadows from fifty years ago. To be in the midst of that small city neighborhood is to experience fully how utterly and totally inexplicable the mystery of Beverly Potts still remains. After one of the largest police investigations in Cleveland history and a Seltzer-led media barrage, after more than half a century of almost continual local notoriety marked by periodic outbursts of renewed official interest and activity, we still know so little. Until the Sheppards' Bay Village home eclipsed it in 1954, Halloran Park ranked as Cleveland's most notorious crime scene. But after all these years, we still don't know the exact nature of the crime or even if it was actually committed in Halloran Park, let alone who the perpetrator or perpetrators may have been. She was just gone.

The national statistics are both numbing and frightening. According to the U.S. Department of Justice, 800,000 children are reported missing, on average, every year. That breaks down to approximately 2,000 a day. Every forty seconds a child disappears somewhere in the United States. Close to 75 percent of those cases may be classified as abandoned children or runaways. More than 25 percent of that number—close to 58,000—are abducted every year. Today, the National Center for Missing and Exploited Children divides cases of child abduction into three broad categories: family (49 percent), acquaintance (27 percent), and stranger (24 percent). Each category is further broken down into such areas as profiles of typical victims and predators, relationship between victim and predator, times of day when kidnapping is most likely to occur, locations where abduction usually takes place, degree of violence employed, use of a weapon, and the likelihood of the victim's death. Any well-trained law enforcement officer realizes that such statistical categorization is only, at best, one of many available investigative tools—though obviously a very helpful one in skilled professional hands. For example, Beverly's personal profile and the circumstances surrounding her disappearance would point informed, modern-day law enforcement personnel toward a specific kind of predator, thus potentially limiting the pool of suspects and cutting down on the amount of investigative time. And time is crucial. Death in child abduction cases is rare, but if it does take place, it will usually occur within three hours of the initial crime. Unfortunately, in late 1951 Cleveland police did not enjoy the benefits of such a sophisticated and systematic breakdown. Therefore, though their investigation into Beverly's disappearance was certainly far more than merely competent and professional by the standards of the day, it lacked a degree of focus. In military terms, it resembled a massive frontal assault rather than a series of precise blitzkrieg attacks. Cleveland police vigorously pursued every lead, no matter how trivial, and every suspect, no matter how unlikely. It is abundantly clear from the surviving police reports that as time went on, the scope of the investigation broadened rather than narrowed. It seems that for years authorities looked into a possible Beverly Potts connection with every sex deviant and molester they corralled. Cleveland police even explored such touchy subjects as what Beverly, her friends, and her classmates knew about the "facts of life" and how much childish exploration may have been going on behind neighborhood garages. It is obvious, however, from the newspaper coverage and the surviving official documentation that the investigation did embrace all three abduction categories as outlined by the National Center for Missing and Exploited Children.

Almost from the day she vanished, there have been conspiratorial musings that Beverly had been spirited away for some sort of unspecified, selfish purpose by someone either in or connected to the Potts family. The police files on the Potts case contain an impressively detailed breakdown of all the relatives on both sides of the family, listing both their relationship to either Robert or Elizabeth and their current addresses. Police reports indicate that those Potts-Treuer relatives over whom hovered the merest whiff of suspicion—and even the vaguest hint of a rumor was sufficient to attract official attention—were subjected to particularly intense scrutiny. Elizabeth Potts's cousin Betty Morbito lived with the family at 11304 Linnet, and police explored the notion that she may have been responsible for Beverly's disappearance because she wanted to raise the child on her own. They gave up the idea after checking her financial records and learning that she did not have the funds to support herself and a child.

Today, standard operating procedure holds that in cases of child abduction and murder, police look first at those in the household closest to the victim. From the surviving evidence, it remains difficult to be certain whether such was the case fifty years ago, but it is clear that police interviewed Beverly's parents and sister repeatedly. Ironically, it was probably this thoroughness on the part of authorities that first raised the possibility in the public mind that someone in the Potts home may have been responsible for whatever happened to her. Police administered lie-detector tests to each person in the household individually, and when technical difficulties rendered the results of those tests useless, authorities questioned the four family members in the home again, this time under strictest security. Police simply arrived unannounced and escorted whichever individual they had decided to retest to an undisclosed location for questioning. The residents of Linnet Avenue certainly knew about these intense double examinations. Undoubtedly, they also picked up at least bits and pieces of the story about Robert Potts having dispatched his daughter and buried her in the basement that newspaper reporters had concocted as a joke and passed on to authorities. The sight of police officers coming to the Potts home repeatedly to give it yet another top-to-bottom search no doubt intensified whatever suspicions may have been lurking in the minds of the Pottses' neighbors. Add to this unsavory mix the fact that many in the neighborhood did not know Robert Potts very well because of his erratic work schedule at the Allen Theater. Though Beverly was, in the words of one police report, "the apple of her father's eye," vague, unsubstantiated allegations that there may have been a dark side to Robert Potts flickered through the Linnet Avenue neighborhood, thus, perhaps, providing the morbidly suspicious with a plausible explanation as to why Beverly was reportedly so shy around men and older boys. Police, of course, checked into this tangle of innuendo as thoroughly as possible, and Robert Potts emerged from their scrutiny essentially untainted. According to official reports, among those who vouched for him under police questioning was L. E. Burden, a movie-projector operator (most likely at the Allen Theater), who assured authorities he knew Robert Potts well, that he drank with him and found him to be happy with his home life and very proud of his family.

Nothing in the relationships among those living in the Potts household would point to a family abduction. In such cases, parents are usually divorced, separated, or have some prior history of open conflict, especially over the child; the would-be abductor has generally issued some sort of threat on the order of "You'll never see your child again"; the abductor is often unemployed or mentally ill, has few ties to the community, and may suspect the child is being sexually or physically abused by the other parent. None of these scenarios are even remotely applicable to the Potts family.

Because of the repeated insistence on the part of all who knew her that Beverly was extremely shy around men and boys—even those she knew—it would, perhaps, seem most likely that she was a victim of acquaintance abduction. In such cases, the kidnapping is invariably accompanied by another crime: robbery or physical or sexual assault. In fact, the abduction serves as the means for creating circumstances favorable to the commission of the accompanying crime. The fact that Beverly literally seemed to vanish from the neighborhood would definitely indicate an acquaintance abduction. (The likelihood of violence is higher in acquaintance abduction than in either of the other two categories.) Perpetrators are usually juveniles, and their victims tend to be teenage girls. (Though only ten, Beverly was tall for her age. Police circulars at the time pointed out that she could easily pass for twelve.) The known characteristics of acquaintance abduction would clearly point the finger of suspicion at someone in the neighborhood, perhaps even on Linnet Avenue itself. But who? If Beverly was as shy as reports insist, she would have been wary in the presence of any adult male, even the father of one of her friends. Could that mean a male authority figure whom she would automatically trust? Someone like a policeman, a fireman, even a priest or minister? A boy her own age would hardly have the strength to "abduct" her without creating a commotion that would attract attention.

The known circumstances surrounding Beverly's disappearance also conform closely to instances of stranger abduction. In such cases, school-age girls (eleven years and older) rather than teens tend to be the likely targets; and they remain victims of opportunity—someone chosen at random rather than someone the perpetrator has previously stalked. And the circumstances on the night of August 24 would make a stranger abduction seem likely. A chance encounter with a young girl walking home alone after dark, somewhat detached from the rest of the crowd, could provide a temptingly ideal opportunity for a potential perpetrator on the prowl. It would hardly be surprising if such a person walked among the show-goers that night at Halloran Park; in fact, an entertainment aimed at youngsters would undoubtedly attract would-be pedophiles or abductors, ranging from those who simply hang around children in order to watch them to those who harbor far more dangerous intentions. Even though no one at the park expected anything out of the ordinary, the police still reaped an impressive tally of reports about unusual or suspicious behavior from show attendees.

In cases of stranger abduction, the crime is more likely to occur in the evening than during the day and within one quarter mile of the victim's home. Beverly disappeared sometime between 9:00 P.M. and 10:00 P.M. within a five-minute walk of her house. Today, the average perpetrator in stranger abduction would be defined as a "social marginal"—a twenty-seven-year-old male, often unemployed, who lives either alone or with his parents and has a record of prior arrests. This description and variations of it could easily be applied to almost anyone in the collection of "perverts," hot-rodders, and social misfits that Cleveland police rounded up in the first weeks of their investigation. There were, perhaps, persons living in the Linnet Avenue neighborhood answering this description, but Beverly's shyness and caution again become major stumbling blocks. If she were shy around men she knew, her sense of danger would increase tenfold around a stranger, even a teenager.

Though extremely unlikely, the notion that Beverly may have simply run off, either alone or with someone else, still persists. Even at the time of her disappearance, however, Cleveland police dismissed such a possibility. None of her clothes were missing; her piggy bank remained untouched; she had even left her dish-washing wages for the evening behind when she and Patsy hopped on their bicycles and headed for the park. In spite of the multitude of bogus Beverly sightings all over Cuyahoga County and beyond, police never unearthed a shred of evidence that suggested she did not plan to return home. (Elizabeth Potts's cousin Betty Morbito insisted Beverly planned to be home early because of the planned outing to Euclid Beach Park the next day, and Fred Krause reported that he, indeed, saw her walking toward the West 117–Linnet Avenue intersection when the show ended.) And there was nothing for her to run away from. Though family affairs may not always have been rosy, a thorough, invasive probing into life in the Potts household on the part of the police failed to uncover any deep, hidden secrets that would prompt a shy and cautious ten-year-old to run away.

The conspiratorially minded familiar with the Potts case find the notion that Beverly could still be alive exceptionally attractive—almost as if she were living in some sort of bizarre witness-protection program. On the one hand, it is impossible to believe that if she had really been alive all these years, she would allow her family and best friend to endure the pain and uncertainty of her sudden disappearance for so long. On the other hand, speculations and suggestions involving possible amnesia hovered around the Beverly Potts investigation almost from the beginning. Once a cliché plotline of old Hollywood, the story has recently also become a staple of made-for-television movies, soap operas, and romance novels. An attractive, young woman of fragile personality goes about the predictable routines of her mundane life—the unglamorous job, the tiny apartment where she lives alone, and the small circle of casual rather than close friends (none of them male). All her life she has been plagued by recurring dreams of people she does not recognize in her waking life; and, though these visions from her subconscious hardly qualify as full-blown nightmares, there is something about them she has always found troubling. The frequency and intensity of the dreams suddenly increase to a disturbing degree; and to alleviate the growing psychological pressure, the woman seeks out the help of a compassionate mental-health professional who eventually leads her to the realization that she had been kidnapped as a child and raised by people not her parents. The haunting faces that pass through her dreams belong to her biological parents and other family members tied to the brief period of her life that predates the kidnapping. While working on this book, I have been asked several times, could something like this have happened to Beverly Potts? In other words, is Cleveland's most famous missing child living out her life somewhere totally unaware of who she really is? Some of those musings have taken a more psychologically complex form: could Beverly, now in her sixties, be living in a mental institution somewhere, suffering from multiple-personality disorder? Rather like the famous 1960s case of Sybil, could she have been so viciously and repeatedly traumatized at some early point in her life following her disappearance that her basic personality fragmented into a number of pieces—that whatever memories she may retain of her life prior to August 24, 1951, lie preserved in the mind of one of her alternate personalities as something that happened to someone else? Until very recently, my stock reply was, "Beverly was ten years, not ten months old." I assumed that at ten years of age she would have possessed far too many memories of people and events to be so completely brainwashed, that there would have been far too much written on her slate for it to be wiped so clean. I have been informed, however, by several mental-health professionals that, given the nature of the brain's wiring at the age of ten, such a scenario does remain possible if not entirely probable.

I sat with Robert Wolf at his dining-room table in January 2003 downing cups of coffee and studying a map of the Halloran Park–Linnet Avenue neighborhood. After a couple hours of detailed analysis and conversation, he tucked his hands in his jean pockets and leaned back in his chair. His forehead wrinkled into a frown; his eyes narrowed into slits; his voice became methodical and even. Slowly, he laid out the various explanations for the events on the night of August 24, 1951; with careful, reasoned deliberation, he separated the improbable scenarios from the more plausible. Given the short distance to her home, it remains very doubtful that Beverly would have ever accepted a ride from anyone. Given her shyness and apparent sense of caution, it is highly unlikely she would have talked with anyone, even someone she knew, in an automobile. It is not entirely clear how large the gathering at Halloran Park may have been at any specific moment in time; it is also not clear how and when the crowd began to disperse. No one, however, even those who thought they saw her talking to someone in a car, admitted to seeing anything unusual. James McArthur agonized over the question of why so many show attendees saw so little, but perhaps that seemingly odd set of circumstances should not come as a surprise. Friday,

August 24, only became significant and memorable through hindsight. No one at Halloran Park that night expected a tragedy; no one would have been on the lookout for anything out of the ordinary. Beverly Potts was simply another neighborhood youngster at a Showagon performance, one among, perhaps, hundreds. Why would anyone, even her acquaintances, take any special note of her? Why would there have been any reason for Fred Krause to give more than a casual glance at the girl he passed on his bicycle as he headed home?

Whatever happened to Beverly Potts either occurred when she was alone or was seemingly so innocuous that no one among the legions of the homeward-bound noticed. If she was violently abducted against her will by a stranger, either a customer leaving Walter's Bar on the corner of West 117 and Linnet or someone cruising the streets in an automobile, that act had to occur at a time when and a place where she would have been relatively isolated. Given the reported circumstances, that allows for only an exceedingly small window of opportunity, if any at all. Once having seized her, however, a potentially violent molester would get her out of the immediate area as quickly and unobtrusively as possible. But, again, no one saw or heard anything suspicious. And no body was ever found. A stranger with no ties to his victim would probably dispose of the corpse in an isolated spot, but he would not necessarily take extraordinary precautions to conceal it. An acquaintance or someone living in the Linnet Avenue neighborhood, however, would do everything possible to make sure the body remained hidden. As Wolf carefully stripped away the unlikely suppositions, an utterly simple, logical, and truly chilling scenario began to loom—perhaps the best explanation we will ever have for what really happened to Beverly Potts on that fateful night of August 24, 1951: a chance encounter, either at Halloran Park or on the way home, with someone she knew well or trusted completely—man, woman, policeman, clergyman, teenager, even a child close to her own age—whose presence would not set off the slightest alarm in Beverly's mind; a detour in her walk home—perhaps up a driveway or across a yard—but one so ordinary, so commonplace, that no one took any notice; a bit of horseplay gone terribly wrong or a violent act of some sort—perhaps deliberate, perhaps accidental, but certainly fatal and in a spot where no one would see; a decision on the part of someone—the perpetrator or someone else—to cover up the evidence. "Somebody! Somebody saw something. Somebody in that neighborhood knew something," declares retired reporter Doris O'Donnell Beaufait

Anita Potts Georges had this memorial stone for her sister placed at the foot of her parents' graves in 1991—a gesture that represents the only form of closure the Potts family has experienced in more than fifty years. Photo by Robert Wolf, courtesy of the Cleveland Police Department.

emphatically. Anita Potts remembers that several weeks into the investigation, a detective (she does not recall who) told her that if Beverly had been snatched by a neighbor, her body probably would not be found until the houses were bulldozed. In an eerie echo of that fifty-year-old speculation, Robert Wolf muses quietly, "All the garages in those days had dirt floors. She could still be somewhere in that neighborhood."

A single headstone marks the spot where Robert and Elizabeth Potts rest side by side in one of Cleveland's older city cemeteries. A few feet below their graves, a simple stone marker lies nestled in the grass; the engraving on its surface reads IN MEMORY OF BEVERLY ROSE POTTS. When Anita had this touching memorial to her sister placed there in 1991, she left instructions that if Beverly's remains are ever discovered and identified, they should find their final resting place in this quiet spot, close to their parents. If that ever comes to pass, the darkness will lift from at least a part of the mystery; and the prayers her family, friends, and classmates offered up more than a half century ago will finally be answered: Beverly Potts will be safely home.

One of the last photographs of Beverly Potts. This picture was taken in Hudson, Ohio, at the home of Edward and Irene (Elizabeth Potts's first cousin) Carney, on Sunday, August 19, 1951. Five days later, Beverly was gone. It remains one of only a couple of photos that show her with her braids cut. This picture—as well as at least one other taken at the time—was not immediately available to Cleveland police when Beverly vanished, because they had not yet been developed. Robert Potts picked up the prints a week or so after his daughter disappeared and turned them over to authorities. Copies were made for the media, but to this day the original prints remain in the voluminous Beverly Potts case files at the Cleveland Police Department. *Cleveland Press* Archives, Cleveland State University.

NOTES

The profiles of child abductors and their victims can be found on the National Center for Missing and Exploited Children's Web site (www.missingkids.com).

Many of the quotations attributed to Anita Potts are drawn from the unedited tape of Mark Wade Stone's November 2003 interview. The draft of Elizabeth Potts's letter to the Metropolitan Life Insurance Company is in the possession of Anita Potts. It remains uncertain whether or not the finished letter was ever sent.

Bibliographical Note

The police files on Beverly Potts's disappearance remain the only major source of information on the case outside of the newspaper coverage and eyewitness testimony. I was allowed access to this material by the police department during the first four months of calendar year 2003. The files consist of four large boxes, each approximately a yard long. One box contains the original material, dating from 1951 to 1955. Some of this documentation has been organized in file folders; a substantial part of it is simply loose. The daily police reports make up the vast majority of this material.

Unfortunately, there are gaps; much of the material is missing. Many of the reports that remain have been stapled together in packets of approximately thirty documents. The rationale for this arrangement is not apparent; different copies of an identical report can be found distributed among two or three different bundles. This box also contains original photographs of Beverly supplied by the Potts family, departmental directives from James McArthur, letters to and from other official agencies, official reports covering isolated phases of the investigation from the 1970s through the 1990s, and a large quantity of loose material (lists of Potts family members, photographs of automobiles, and what can only be described as random notes, as well as material that defies easy categorization). The other three boxes contain material gathered by Robert Wolf during his eighteen-month investigation in 2000–2001: aerial photographs of the Halloran Park-Linnet Avenue neighborhood, city maps, photographs taken by Wolf of locations relevant to the case, and other material related to his search for the writer of the Larkin letters, such as lists of *Plain Dealer* subscribers in the Linnet Avenue area.

The Cleveland Police Historical Society Museum possesses only two documents related to the Beverly Potts investigation. Patrolman Raymond Mickol's notebook was donated to the museum collection by his family on January 17, 2003. It was assigned the catalogue number 2003.005.001. The copy of the police circular featuring Beverly's photograph and containing a detailed description, including her dental records, was discovered in a box of loose, disorganized material by museum personnel in early 2003. It was immediately turned over to me for incorporation in this book. As of publication, this valuable record of the Potts investigation has not been assigned an official catalogue number.

OTHER SOURCES

Cleveland News. August–November 1951; September 1952; December 1955; August 1958.

Cleveland Plain Dealer. August–November 1951. September 1952; December 1955; August 1957; August 1958; July–August 1960; August 1961; April 1962; January 1973; April 1973; August 1980; January 1988; February 1994; August 2000–August 2001.

Cleveland Press. August–November 1951; September 1952; December 1955; November 1958; July 1960; April 1962; April 1973; August 1973; August 1980.

National Center for Missing and Exploited Children Web site. www.missing kids.com. Accessed October 3–6, 2003.

Index